Melvin F. Kendrick

D0463848

History is about building bridges between the past and the present, observing both banks of the river, taking an active part on both sides...

Bernhard Schlink, from *The Reader*, 1997

The Accidental Captives

The Story of Seven Women
Alone in Nazi Germany

CAROLYN GOSSAGE

with the cooperation of Peter Levitt

MJF BOOKS
New York

Published by MJF Books
Fine Communications
322 Eighth Avenue
New York, NY 10001

The Accidental Captives
LC Control Number: 2015933101
ISBN 978-1-60671-308-2

English-language edition first published by
I.B. Tauris & Co Ltd in the United Kingdom.

This edition is published by MJF Books in arrangement with Dundurn Press.

Printed in the United States of America.

MJF Books and the MJF colophon are trademarks of
Fine Creative Media, Inc.

QF   10   9   8   7   6   5   4   3   2   1

Contents

Preface and acknowledgements

This book owes its genesis to a chance discovery made over twenty years ago in the Metro Toronto Reference Library. I was sifting through the library's card catalogue researching another project entirely when I stumbled upon *Free Trip to Berlin*, published in Canada in 1943.

The book's unusual title immediately caught my attention, and once I had a copy in my hands it was a matter of minutes before I was irrevocably drawn into this extraordinary and fascinating story. Almost certainly this was largely due to the author's distinctive style. Isabel Russell Guernsey was clearly a woman of exceptional intelligence, wit and charm, whose irrepressible *joie de vivre* reverberated through the decades since the publication of her book.

In April 1941, Isabel Guernsey was a passenger on board the *Zamzam*, an Egyptian liner sailing from New York Harbour to Cape Town, when the ship was attacked and sunk by a German raider in the South Atlantic. The *Zamzam*'s two hundred passengers were literally fished out of the water by the crew of the raider and transported via a German prison ship to Vichy France. Here the majority of them – as neutral citizens of the United States – were then released, while the remaining passengers were transported to the Third Reich as prisoners of war. Among these were 28 women and children who were citizens of either Great Britain or British Commonwealth countries – including Isabel Guernsey and a number of other Canadians – who were dispatched by train through

German-occupied France and zigzagged their way through Nazi Germany before arriving at Liebenau, an internment camp in the vicinity of Lake Constance (the Bodensee), near the Swiss border.

Three months later, seven of the Canadian women who had been passengers on board the *Zamzam* received permission to leave the camp and travel unescorted to Berlin, where they held high hopes that arrangements for their safe return to Canada could be made within a matter of weeks. Instead, before their exchange for an equal number of German women in Canada was finally realised, they remained stranded in Berlin for the better part of a year.

By the time I closed the covers of Isabel Guernsey's book, I realised that I had unwittingly fallen under its spell. What an intriguing story and what an incredible journey! I was consumed with curiosity, but soon realised that I was also left with more questions than answers. Isabel's account concentrated primarily on her recollections of the people she came to know during her stay in Germany, whereas her impressions of the six Canadian women who shared the same experience remained on the periphery. Isabel herself mentions this disparity in her foreword to *Free Trip to Berlin*. 'I regret that my *Zamzam* companions appear so incidentally in these pages, which is a pity, since each one is a story in herself... This is a story mostly about people – people I met and grew to know in Germany. My hope is simply that they, through me, may shed a little light that hasn't been shed before.'

I, too, found myself equally disappointed that her companions in adversity were mentioned only in passing. Dozens of beguiling questions had already begun to surface and percolate in the back of my mind. Who were these six other Canadian women who had been thrown together by fate and circumstance as Isabel's companions on this 1941–42 wartime odyssey that ended with them being marooned in Berlin? Vida Steele from Three Hills, Alberta, Olga Guttormson of Naicam, Saskatchewan, Allison 'Jamie' Henderson of Winnipeg, Manitoba, Katharine 'Kitsi' Strachan and Doreen Turner from Toronto and Clara Guilding, formerly of Toronto. Why had they chosen to leave the safety of home to risk a four-week Atlantic crossing fraught with uncertainty and danger? How had they reacted – both individually and collectively – to the countless difficulties they encountered on their long and wearisome odyssey? And after spending more than a year in Nazi Germany, initially as civilians detained in a variety of jails, then an internment camp and later as 'enemy aliens' at large in Berlin, how had they dealt with the challenges of fending for themselves and organising their lives in the war-torn capital of the Third Reich?

In retrospect, it must have been at precisely this moment that I realised that sooner or later I would have to try to find answers to these and other enticing questions in order to record my own expanded version of this long-forgotten and little-known World War II episode.

When their ship was sunk from under them in the South Atlantic by the *Atlantis* in April 1941, there began a series of shared adventures which included 140 Americans – their fellow passengers on board the *Zamzam*. Ultimately, protected by their neutrality, the Americans were destined for release; however, for the Canadians the journey had barely begun.

Now it would be up to me to attempt to shed even more light on what lay beyond Isabel's personal perspective. However, it was only four years ago that I began concentrating my efforts on finding answers to the myriad unrelenting questions that had remained with me since my discovery of *Free Trip to Berlin* more than twenty years earlier. It was now or never!

Since Isabel's original account had been written long before the final outcome of World War II, as an aspiring journalist she had taken pains to protect the identity of certain individuals she encountered during her time in

Berlin. In many cases, she made a point of identifying these people using only their first names. Her intentions were noble, but this inevitably created certain difficulties in terms of further research.

Fortunately, another of her *Zamzam* companions, missionary-nurse Olga Guttormson had written and published *Ships Will Sail Again*, which includes her own detailed account of the Canadians' extended stay in the Third Reich. Although a few of the others left cursory references and reminiscences of their mutual ordeal, without the literary legacy of these two women there would be little or nothing to bear witness to the relatively brief presence of these Canadian women in Berlin. What they have written – each from her own point of view – presents the reader with a first-hand account of life among the inhabitants of Berlin between September 1941 and June 1942. Events observed, almost seventy years ago, through the eyes of outsiders looking in.

In any case, most of the additional side bars only came to light once I had decided that I would have to cast the net wider by sending out an author's query to local newspapers across Canada in an attempt to locate survivors or relatives of those who had been passengers on board the ill-fated *Zamzam*. The response to this was nothing short of overwhelming, and provided me with invaluable new information and insights from a variety of sources across Canada, and also the United States. Among these were the colourful revelations found in the letters of Kathleen Levitt, a young British war-guest who had wisely decided to remain in the Liebenau internment camp with her two young children, Peter and Wendy, rather than risk the perils of accompanying her Canadian friends to Berlin. Then, too, there were the exhilarating first-hand reports and photographs of two American journalists, David Scherman and Charles Murphy, both of whom had been released in Biarritz with the other American citizens after an extended five-week ordeal aboard the German prison ship *Dresden* as involuntary guests of the Third Reich.

As for the seven Canadian women in Berlin who had been unwilling participants in this wartime drama, their experiences and observations, hopes and frustrations struck me – even for those exceptional times – as something unique and extraordinary. Each had been caught up unbidden and unexpectedly in a war in which they became reluctant pawns in a diplomatic game of cat-and-mouse.

Once dispatched to Hitler's stronghold, the seven Canadian Zamzamers also became, by default, an unrecognised and inconsequential addition to Berlin's population, sharing the same cares and anxieties, withstanding the same miseries and misfortunes while, at the same time, remaining outsiders in an alien place. By the same token, as 'enemy' foreigners caught up in unfamiliar surroundings and unusual circumstances, each had the benefit of her own unique perspectives and personal insights. And the more of these I discovered, the more fascinated I became as the pieces of the story of this incredible journey gradually fell into place.

In closing, I can only hope that others will find this virtually unknown and untold fragment in the vast kaleidoscope of history – as observed from within and without – a source of similar fascination.

***

And I now, with great pleasure, extend my sincere gratitude to all those who contacted me in response to my request for information about the last voyage of the *Zamzam* and the odyssey of the 'Canadian Seven'. Without their enthusiastic response, the contents of this book would have been greatly diminished. In particular I wish to acknowledge the contribution of Peter Levitt of Toronto, a *Zamzam* survivor, who was among the first to contact me and has provided me with a wealth of material, including his mother's letters and his own childhood memories of his adventures on the high seas and internment in Germany.

I am also greatly indebted to Janet Steele of San Jose, California and other members of Vida Steele's family, including Vera Steele Hazelton of Three Hills, Alberta, for all their help and encouragement; to Marlene Leicht and Garth Ulrich of Naicam, Saskatchewan for generously providing me with Olga Guttormson's memoirs and other previously inaccessible material, as well as to Zamzam survivor Eleanor Danielson Anderson of Lindsborg, Kansas for her helpful assistance; to Katharine 'Kitsi' Strachan's late brother, Don Neelands of Toronto and to her daughter and son-in-law, Janet and David Cameron of Millbrook, Ontario, as well as Irma Coucill of Toronto for their interest and hospitality. Thank you, too, to Marvin Demuth of Arkansas for the information he provided concerning Rev. Fred Henderson and his wife, Allison 'Jamie' Henderson of Winnipeg, Manitoba; also to Christopher Hives of the University of British Columbia Archives in Vancouver for hunting down useful material related to Isabel Russell Guernsey and her geologist husband, Tarrant.

To John Scherman of New York, for his kind permission to refer to and quote from the unpublished memoirs of his father, renowned *Life* magazine photographer David Scherman, a warm thank you. Likewise to Wendy Wright – she, whose keyboarding and translation skills are without equal – for her extensive contribution and encouragement. Particular thanks, as well, to Frau Hilga Sandkamp, her good friend in Hamburg for sharing the story of Kapitänleutnant Lorenz Kasch of the Hilfskreuzer *Atlantis*. And a special tip of the hat to my friend, Senator Nancy Ruth for graciously providing me with a welcome roof over my head during my research visits in Ottawa.

The interest and assistance of Paulette Dozois of the National Archives of Canada can only be described as exceptional. By the same token, her equally helpful counterpart, Frau Lucia van der Linde of the Politischen Archiv des Auswärtigen Amt in Berlin, gave new meaning to the word efficiency. Thank you both for all your efforts on my behalf. Also my thanks to Tim Dube and Melanie Quintal of the National Archives of Canada for pointing me in the right direction and to Herr Dr Axel Wittenburg of Freiburg for his painstaking research at the German Military Archives there, in addition to the obliging co-operation of Franz Goettlinger and Angelika Nauroth of the Bundesarchiv; Karen Baumhoff and Markus Toth of Ullstein Bild and Sabine Kalkmann of the Adlon Kempinski Hotel in Berlin.

But the full weight of my eternal gratitude belongs in the laps (and laptops) of Dr Britta Grell and Dr Stephan Lahrem for their unstinting efforts with the German translation and editing of the original manuscript published by Christoph Links Verlag, Berlin in 2009. During their extended stay here in Toronto, we frequently burned the midnight oil, fine-tuning the text and generally enjoying the many hours spent together in total harmony. Such a pleasure! Likewise, I want to extend my sincere thanks, as well, to the I.B.Tauris team and most particularly to Joanna Godfrey and Gretchen Ladish for all their hard work in making this publication a reality.

And last – but by no means least – my loving thanks to Mike and to my children, Valerie and Graeme, whose encouragement and support have carried me through from start to finish.

Carolyn Gossage
Toronto, April 2011

1

The last voyage of the *Zamzam*
20 March–17 April 1941

Welcome on board

When you are six, certain events become etched in your mind's eye for all time. For young Peter Levitt, one of these defining flashbacks from his childhood is that of his mother, Kathleen Levitt, shepherding him and his younger sister, Wendy, up the gangplank to board the SS *Zamzam* in New York Harbour on 20 March 1941. Having spent a wretched winter in Montreal, Kathleen Levitt, a British evacuee, had made up her mind that – come what may – she was prepared to face the wartime perils of an Atlantic crossing to reunite the children with their father, who had been posted to South Africa as an instructor with the Royal Air Force.

To the ears of six-year-old Peter, the ship's name – *Zamzam* – sounded quite exotic, and it was only many years later that he learned that her Egyptian owners – the Alexandria Steam and Navigation Company – had chosen it because of its reference to a sacred well in Islam's holy city of Mecca.[1] The shipping company which owned the *Zamzam* had evidently engaged the services of the highly reputable Thomas Cook and Sons travel agency to drum up business for the vessel's return journey from New York to Alexandria and – even on short notice – the agency's assurances of a safe passage aboard a neutral ship had proven to be remarkably successful. Just over two hundred travellers had unwittingly signed on for the voyage of a lifetime.

Once on board, Kathleen and the children were ushered to their quarters, and soon became acquainted with the two Canadian women in the adjoining cabin – Isabel Guernsey and Katharine 'Kitsi' Strachan. Like Kathleen, both Isabel and Kitsi had made the same decision and chosen to take their chances on a lengthy voyage to join their husbands after months of separation. Isabel, who was in her mid-thirties, held a master's degree in French from the University of British Columbia, and exuded the confidence that is the usual by-product of a higher education and a privileged background. From her, Kathleen learned that Isabel had been in Vancouver on home leave from Rhodesia, where her geologist husband was a consultant to the Anglo-American Corporation of South Africa. Although, as members of the upper crust of Canadian society, both Kitsi and Isabel shared similarly affluent backgrounds, Kitsi had grown up in Toronto and was appreciably younger. Having been married barely two years earlier she was yearning to be reunited with her husband, Robin, who was currently on assignment in Aden with the British Colonial Office.

As the new-found friends chatted and explored their less-than-inviting First Class accommodations, which included a shared bathroom, the other passengers were gradually making their way up the gangplank of the aging liner with obvious trepidation. To a casual observer the sight could well have conjured up a vision vaguely reminiscent of the beasts venturing onto Noah's Ark. The process of boarding had been interminably long and fraught with delay. Patience was in short supply and tempers were becoming increasingly frayed. To make matters worse, the weather had turned miserably cold, and a bone-chilling March wind was sweeping the length of the harbour.

From the bridge, Captain William Gray Smith gazed down with a distinctly jaundiced eye at the wind-blown passengers left shivering on the pier of Hoboken Harbour. Having safely negotiated his ship on a lengthy journey from Alexandria carrying Jewish refugees from Germany to a safe haven in America, he was now faced with the daunting prospect of a return voyage to Egypt by way of the Cape of Good Hope bearing what could only be described as a motley assortment of passengers.[2]

The bulk of those restlessly waiting to come on board were American and Canadian missionaries – including priests, teachers, nurses, doctors, wives and mothers with children in tow. Between them, they represented over twenty different religious denominations and all were bound for Cape Town and from there into the Dark Continent to shine the Light of the Lord wherever they had been called to serve. Small wonder, then, that the ship would quickly become unofficially dubbed 'the missionary ship', since their number comprised roughly seventy-five per cent of the passengers whose lives depended on Captain Smith's ability to bring them safely to their destinations on the other side of the ocean.[3]

In the spring of 1941, the Battle of the Atlantic was continuing to threaten all of the main shipping lanes. However, the Zamzam – flying its neutral flag – would follow a more southerly and presumably safer route, with only the remotest possibility of an encounter with a marauding German U-boat or raider. Ironically, many of these one hundred and forty missionaries – Lutherans, Catholics, Seventh Day Adventists and Baptists – boarding the Zamzam along with their household possessions and cars were journeying to Central Africa as volunteer replacements for their German missionary counterparts, who had been interned there by the British.

Among the missionaries on board, Canada was represented by four women of various religious denominations: Vida Steele from Three Hills, Alberta, who was accompanying her husband, Ellsworth; Olga Guttormson of Naicam, Saskatchewan; Allison 'Jamie' Henderson, wife of Dr Alfred Henderson, both of whom hailed from Winnipeg, Manitoba; and lastly Clara Guilding, originally a Torontonian, who was accompanying her husband Rev. W.J. Guilding, based in Detroit.

Also on the passenger list were Rev. William Edwards, who, with his wife and son, were survivors of the *Athenia*, the first Allied passenger ship to be sunk by a German submarine – U-30 on 3 September 1939, within hours of Britain and France's declaration of war on Germany. Their destination was the Congo, where they had spent thirty years in the mission fields.

Missionaries aside, there was a second – and perhaps equally perplexing – addition to the mix, a group of two dozen irreverent and boisterous young volunteer ambulance drivers, most of them the sons of affluent American families. They had signed on with the British–American Ambulance Corps to serve with General de Gaulle's Free French troops in North Africa. Their vehicles and equipment had already been stowed on board, and their enthusiasm and high spirits knew no bounds. From Captain Smith's standpoint this unlikely conglomeration of devout Christian missionaries and rowdy roustabouts had all the makings of an additional and entirely unwelcome headache.

As the missionaries' fervent hymns wafted up to him from the pier, the doughty Captain Smith, who at 51 was a weathered veteran of countless crossings, muttered prophetically to his fellow Scot, First Engineer John Burns, 'Mark my words, Chief. It's bad luck for a ship to have so many Bible punchers and sky pilots aboard. No good will come of this.'[4]

In addition to this dubious combination, there were six Southern businessmen from North Carolina's tobacco industry who had responded to an appeal by the British government to set up a tobacco auction system in Salisbury, Rhodesia. They were part of a relatively small number of non-aligned travellers that included several other British and Canadian wives en route to join their husbands, two Greek nurses returning home after receiving their training in New York and James de Graaf Hunter, the former chief of the India Geological Survey, who was accompanied by his wife and daughter. Then there was an elderly British doctor and his wife, who had opted to exchange the perils of the London Blitz for a new life in southern Africa, a Belgian family of three, and finally a rather enigmatic figure – a young Italian prince who claimed to be emigrating to South Africa.

Aside from Captain Smith and his chief engineer, with a few exceptions, such as the ship's Greek stewardess, the *Zamzam*'s crew was almost entirely Egyptian. Having made the long and hazardous journey from Alexandria to New York without incident, in spite of snow on the deck and the generally foul weather, the crew's spirits were running high. Within hours they would be homeward bound, and by virtue of their ship's name the protection of Allah was all but guaranteed. What the future held in store for them would, unfortunately, require a good deal more than misplaced faith.

By midnight, the *Zamzam* had cast off from her moorings and slipped out of the harbour into the oily swells of the grey Atlantic, steering a southerly course towards Baltimore – her first port of call.

With the onset of daylight, the passengers awakened to the sound of gulls – and people began taking the measure of their ship and its so-called amenities and generally acquainting themselves with its layout. For Kathleen Levitt, it was the beginning of a disenchantment that would grow with each passing day. To begin with, the heating system had malfunctioned and she and the two children had to layer themselves with every bit of warm clothing she could lay her hands on. What's more, there was no water in the bathroom, bells failed to function when rung, and the service rendered by the ship's crew was next to non-existent.

And Kathleen Levitt was far from alone in her observations about the squalid conditions on board the *Zamzam*. The consensus among the hapless passengers was that they had somehow been duped into boarding an ancient rustbucket with a crew whose qualifications were highly questionable; the first of these shortcomings was an apparent inability either to speak or understand more than a few words of pidgin English. The voyage had barely begun and already there was widespread frustration and a sense of common outrage among the passengers.

Within twenty-four hours of her departure from New York Harbour, the *Zamzam* was heading up Chesapeake Bay to Baltimore. Here the ship was scheduled to take on a few more passengers and additional cargo – primarily lubricating oil, which was desperately needed by the British armoured forces in North Africa, and also a quantity of ammonium sulphate – a component in the manufacture of explosives – which was ostensibly being transported overseas for use in Egypt as fertiliser.

To pass the time, the missionaries assembled on the quay to sing a few hymns of praise and the members of the Ambulance Corps attempted to drown them out with their own repertoire of bawdy songs. This brand of deliberate antagonism on the part of the drivers would characterise the relationship between this group of high-spirited young volunteers and the missionary camp for the remainder of the voyage. The fun had barely begun!

From the outset, certain members of the missionary contingent, which far outnumbered the remaining passengers, had expressed their vehement disapproval of the rowdy young ambulance drivers and their rambunctious ways. There were, after all, well over thirty innocent young children on board, who should most certainly be spared exposure to public profanity, to say nothing of drunken and disorderly conduct.

As the *Zamzam* continued to follow her southward course along the American coastline, with each passing day it was becoming increasingly clear that some of the more zealous missionaries were prepared to go to any lengths to try to persuade Captain Smith that it was his Christian duty to close down the ship's bar. His adamant refusal to do so did little to endear him to these righteously indignant supplicants, and the atmosphere on board began to assume the nature of a floating battleground. Sinners on one side and the righteous on the other.

This is not to suggest that the missionaries were – by any stretch of the imagination – living in a state of peace and harmony with one another. In fact, their interdenominational bickering and back-biting had already become a source of constant amusement to the first-class passengers who had been the target of censorious Christian disapproval and tut-tutting ever since the *Zamzam* put to sea.

It would be difficult to improve upon the Victorian novelist Anthony Trollope's interpretation of the state-of-mind that overtakes fellow-travellers who have embarked on a voyage together as total strangers. In his novel *John Caldigate*, Trollope writes,

> There is no peculiar life more thoroughly apart from life in general, more unlike our usual life, more completely a life of itself, governed by its own rules and having its own roughness and amenities, than life aboard ship. What tender friendships it produces and what bitter enmities! How completely the society has formed itself into separate sets after the first three or four days…

As first-class passengers and frequenters of the ship's bar, Kathleen, Isabel and Kitsi were counted among those on the verge of being condemned to eternal damnation along with their shipmates and friends, the six tobacco merchants from

Wilson, North Carolina. Added to this were a few other kindred spirits who also found the consumption of alcoholic beverages a pleasurable pastime. And given the additional burden of prevailing conditions on board, its effects could, in fact, prove downright therapeutic! Nothing like a smart cocktail or a whiskey and soda to soothe the nerves and warm the heart. Mamoud, the Egyptian barman who dispensed drinks from a telephone-booth-sized bar in one corner of the lounge, was only too happy to be of assistance.

In an extract from one of Kathleen's myriad letters, dated 28 March 1941 – their eighth day aboard she wrote,

> Well, this is an adventure…And how! One certainly does strange things in wartime. This is the most extraordinary ship which has ever sailed the seas…Today we are well into the tropics and the humidity is very great. I have seen flying fish and feel very much travelled…[5]

In the mind of her six-year-old son, the daily lessons which some of the missionary teachers had set up for the benefit of the children on board remain a clear and present memory. These lessons also served as something of a relief to the mothers, who were grateful for this break from the constant demands of parenthood. And, in the process of these daily bouts of ship-board schooling, as one of the 34 children on board under the age of 14, Peter would also hear innumerable Bible stories and, although tone deaf, was enjoined to break into fulsome hymns of heavenly praise.

As the ship slowly proceeded southward from Baltimore to Trinidad, she sailed for several days through the Sargasso Sea at a speed of 8 knots. It was a rare and beautiful experience that moved Isabel Guernsey to rhapsodise over the sight of 'seaweed that produces floating islands of gold in the brilliant blue of the tropical waters'.[6]

Early on the morning of Sunday 29 March – nine days after escaping the wintry blasts of New York – the passengers awakened to find that the ship was dropping anchor about twenty minutes by launch from the quay of Port of Spain. What a relief to be able to set foot on dry land and take advantage of a day in the land of the calypso, enjoying the balmy air and sampling the succulent tropical fruits that were on offer at every turn! After days of being served food that was close to inedible, it came as a most welcome change, and for those who were so inclined ample quantities of celebratory rum punches and cocktails awaited.

To their delight, the Seventh Day Adventist group discovered there was a local Sunday morning Adventist prayer meeting in progress. After a warm welcome, they were invited to join the assembled throng that afternoon, and were driven into the countryside by the mission superintendent to admire the school the Adventists had established there.[7]

For all concerned, this brief stopover in Trinidad had proved a welcome respite from life aboard the *Zamzam*. In fact, as they clambered back on board the passengers felt a universal sense of reluctance at the thought of a return to the discomfort and frustrations they had come to expect. In the small hours of the following morning, having taken on fresh supplies, the decrepit liner weighed anchor and continued southward to refuel in Pernambuco's famed port city of Recife.

As the *Zamzam* passed the mouth of the Amazon the water became muddy and the atmosphere on the ship more sombre. They came upon an empty life raft with the markings of the Blue Star Line. Had the raft belonged to a ship that had been sunk by a German U-boat? The possibility weighed heavily on Captain Smith, and he made the decision to steer his southward course towards Pernambuco with utmost caution and without a glimmer of light. The order for a total blackout became the cause of considerable consternation among his passengers who, until that point, had been harbouring illusions that they were in absolutely no danger of attack – immediate or otherwise. After all, had they not been assured in New York that such a possibility was entirely based on deliberate fear-mongering and was totally without foundation?

Two new passengers

By the time the *Zamzam* arrived in Recife, on Brazil's easternmost tip, the passengers had had ample opportunity to band together and form alliances, but also to discover specific targets of mutual animosity; none was more universal than the general feeling of discontent about the countless inadequacies of the *Zamzam* and the demeanour of her crew. A letter written to relatives by one of the passengers and later confiscated provides a graphic glimpse into the general state of affairs:

> You would really be amazed if you could see the condition of the kitchen here. Dirt is of no object to them. The waiters carry the spoons in their pockets along with their money, handkerchiefs and whatnot. The glasses aren't washed but just refilled and given to somebody else. I'm not at all sure about the dishes and the silver either.[8]

These and similar impressions were quickly conveyed to two newcomers who had been impatiently waiting on the quay to come on board – David Scherman, a young *Life* magazine photographer, and Charles Murphy, a seasoned editor of *Life's* sister publication, *Fortune*. Murphy and Scherman were on assignment to cover the Desert War in North Africa, and had flown down to Brazil from New York via Miami on a Pan American Airlines Clipper in order to shorten their journey.

As journalists, both men were prepared for any eventuality – including delays. However, by the time the *Zamzam* put in to port, they had long since begun to wonder if the ship actually existed. According to Scherman, their initial enquiries about the arrival of the *Zamzam* were met with blank stares. Nobody – including the American consul – had even heard the ship's name, let alone any details relating to its arrival date.[9]

Eventually they located a Norwegian shipping agent situated in one of the city's back streets and, after close questioning, he admitted – with some reluctance – that he did, in fact, know of such a vessel, and that it *might* be putting in to the port to take on fuel and water at an unspecified date. After a close look at their passports, the agent revealed to Scherman and Murphy that he had been pestered by no less than thirty mysterious telephone calls concerning the *Zamzam* and that, for reasons of security, information about the date of the vessel's scheduled arrival was definitely not common knowledge. Could this not be a red-flag indicator that the *Zamzam* – a purportedly neutral vessel – had become the object of interest to the large number of German informers and spies whose presence in Pernambuco had been widely recognised for quite some time?

Initially, Murphy, a hard-bitten veteran of the news world, had taken a dim view of these suspicions and was convinced that American neutrality would remain unchallenged. As a survivor of Admiral Byrd's polar expedition, he, for one, was not prepared to be intimidated by inflammatory talk about spies and Nazi sympathisers. Within a matter of days, though, circumstances were to prove that he had perhaps spoken too soon, and Murphy decided it was time to send a radiogram to the captain of the *Zamzam*, position still unknown, advising him of Murphy and Scherman's presence in Pernambuco and hinting that Smith's early arrival would, indeed, be welcomed. Not unexpectedly, no reply was ever received, and it was only weeks later that Captain Smith sheepishly confessed to Murphy, 'I got yurr wire, Charley, but I couldna really answer it, could I now?'[10]

As the *Zamzam* was slowly but surely making its leisurely way towards Recife, Scherman and Murphy were put to the test of trying to make the most of their extended stay there. Comfortably ensconced in the Grande Hotel, they spent their evenings fighting a losing battle at the gaming tables and their days sauntering idly along the wharfs looking for ships that might – by some slim chance – happen to be the long overdue *Zamzam*.

They also quickly discovered that an all-too-obvious German presence in Pernambuco was almost impossible to ignore. Was it simply their imagination that the German room clerk was smiling at them knowingly? Or that strange characters mysteriously disappeared around corners just as they were about to get into the hotel elevator and return to their room? To satisfy their curiosity, one day they deliberately left their room unlocked and placed a few papers in the bottom of a drawer, carefully lined up with pencil marks. On their return, the papers were still in the drawer, but their position was ever so slightly out of alignment. Perhaps it had just been the chamber maid? But then again there were occasional strange telephone calls to their room – always unidentified – asking when the *Zamzam* was due to arrive. Who were these people that were so anxious to have this information?

After a week of these cat-and-mouse games, both 'norte americanos' were more than ready to be on their way. In a disgruntled letter to his colleagues at *Fortune*, Murphy wrote, 'An American doesn't have to look under his bed to realise that on the Brazilian bulge, the war is closer to this continent than we might have surmised at home.'[11]

Then, one morning, just as they were on the point of despair, the clerk at the hotel desk called out to them, 'Gentlemen, your ship has arrived!' Breakfast was left on the table as Murphy and Scherman made a mad dash for the docks for their first glimpse of their long-awaited ship – a long dark hull listing visibly to starboard. The superstructure was an unappetising shade of brown and the ship's rails were crammed with passengers desperate to disembark. This, then, was the *Zamzam* – well past her prime but still miraculously afloat.

One of the North Carolina tobacco men, Paul Burton, leaned out over the rail and shouted down to the two new arrivals warning them not to come aboard. When they indicated that they were prepared to take their chances, Burton pointed up at the ship's thin smokestack with its two Arabic characters and the letters MISR painted underneath and yelled down to them, 'That's what this is – MISR. This here's a misery ship!'

During an exploratory trip ashore, the Southern tobacco merchants and a few of the more fun-loving women – including Kathleen, Kitsi and Isabel – joined forces with Scherman and Murphy and later enjoyed a long and memorable evening of liquidly primed revelry together on the beach – much to the attendant disapproval of some of their hymn-singing missionary shipmates the following morning. By this time, Kathleen, Kitsi and Isabel had long since become fast friends, and within hours of meeting one another, Isabel, the aspiring journalist, and young David Scherman had quickly established an instant and lasting rapport.[12]

The highlight of the *Zamzam*'s departure from Recife Harbour on the morning of 8 April was the sight of a magnificent rainbow – the first of many on this ill-fated crossing to South Africa. The majority of the missionaries were convinced that the rainbow must surely be a sign that the Lord's blessing was upon them; however, their joyful songs of praise were soon dampened by unwelcome news. Passengers were duly informed that blackout conditions would continue to prevail. This had been decreed in accordance with orders received from the British Admiralty during the ship's layover in Pernambuco. Captain Smith's request that his ship travel with all lights burning due to the presence on board of 77 women and over thirty children had been summarily dismissed. Nor were the passengers apprised of the fact that their captain had also been instructed that he must negotiate his way across the South Atlantic following a deliberately pre-arranged course and passing through two specific compass points. The Admiralty had taken the position that since the *Zamzam*'s hold was loaded with British cargo, these decisions were entirely within their purview. Having first set off on an easterly bearing, Smith would have to steer a southerly course in the direction of Sao Paulo before veering back towards the east.[13]

And, true to his profession, magazine photographer Scherman was already busily clicking his cameras' shutters at every possible opportunity. From past experience he had learned that his chosen subjects were not always willing to co-operate with what they perceived to be a prying photographer, but on board the *Zamzam* he was in for a pleasant surprise. Without exception, everyone wanted to be in the picture. They were, after all, part and parcel of a great adventure, and the idea of being immortalised on film was irresistible. Smile … click … smile … click …

A certain indefinable frisson of apprehension had, however, begun to shake the confidence of some of the more observant passengers, although the missionary majority was still labouring under the delusion that the Lord would take care of His own. By the same token, the Muslim crew were equally secure in the knowledge that Allah would protect them and their holy ship in any hour of need.

Ever since the *Zamzam*'s first stop in Baltimore, when the lifeboats were swung out over the water, they had remained suspended there in a state of constant readiness. As a further precaution, one or other of the ship's lifeboat crews held a daily practice drill, and the use of all civilian radios was strictly prohibited in case the ship's position were to be inadvertently revealed to an unknown adversary. The element of danger in the *Zamzam's* passage to Cape Town was slowly but surely becoming undeniable, but for the moment the possibility of an attack remained largely unspoken.

For the children on board, the effect of the blackout was negligible, whereas a number of the adults found it indescribably tiresome and more than a little unsettling. Why, for example, were such extreme precautions being taken on board an unarmed ship flying the flag of a supposedly neutral country? And what was the explanation for the vessel's zigzag course? Not surprisingly, these pressing questions remain unanswered, but Captain Smith's instructions to the passengers left little room for doubt. They were to be followed to the letter and without exception. Not so much as the flicker of a match or the glow of a cigarette would be tolerated on deck. In the lounge, the wiring had been rigged to an automatic switch that cut the light circuit whenever someone opened the door, with the result that reading was next to impossible and conversation – like the light – became an on-again, off-again activity.[14]

Ventilation in the cabins was another perplexing problem. One of the young ambulance drivers, Jim Stewart, divulged the fact that – weather permitting – he and his pals preferred to sleep up on deck. On stormy nights, in an attempt to let in some outside air, they unscrewed their cabin light-bulbs and opened the portholes, but invariably they would find themselves drenched with the rain and seawater that came pouring in. Added to this was a plethora of other trials – overcrowded quarters, bad food and non-stop prayer meetings in the lounge as well as on deck, accompanied at every turn by the ever-present sound of wailing infants and children. Small wonder that the ambulance boys were becoming increasingly restless and disgruntled. In such trying circumstances, what better solution than to soak up their troubles with a few good stiff drinks?

In addition to their ongoing antics with the missionaries, some of the ambulance contingent had also found yet another opportunity to exercise their penchant for amusement at the expense of others. In this instance, the dual target of their ribald attempts at humour came in the form of William Robert, a pampered dachshund, and his doting owner, Mrs Elise Lassetter. Any sighting of Willy, referred to as 'the pet of some and the pest of others'[15] sent up the signal that his mistress was about to heave into view like a ship under full sail. Described by some as fat and jolly, to her detractors – unlike that of her darling Willy – Mrs Lassetter's pedigree was definitely open to question. Claiming marriage to a doctor in South Africa, she affected a frightfully British accent; however, in due course, when the situation demanded that each passenger's citizenship be clearly established, she conveniently produced an American passport from the depths of her handbag.

Although she never mentioned it in her letters, the question of passports had undoubtedly crossed Kathleen Levitt's mind more than once, particularly after the ship began sailing under blackout conditions. Although it remained only a remote possibility, the mere thought of falling into German hands was something to be taken very seriously, for inside each British passport, the holder's religion was included as part of the information provided. In Kathleen's case, it was clearly stated in her passport that she was Jewish. This was a fact she had revealed to no one – not even to Kitsi or Isabel, nor to her devoted admirer, North Carolina tobacco merchant, Harry Cawthorne. But should the need arise, she was fully aware that it was crucial for her own protection and that of her children to dispose of her passport instantly by whatever means necessary.

The first real scare came on the afternoon of 14 April. The *Zamzam*, on a south-easterly heading, suddenly swung abruptly to the west and began heading back in the direction of South America. The chief engineer's orders had been to increase the ship's speed to the maximum. The twin screws were labouring under the strain, and there was a shuddering sensation as the old warhorse pressed forward through the oncoming waves. Towards dusk, the original course was resumed, but a new day dawned before Captain Smith concluded that it was now safe to point his vessel's bow back towards Cape Town. To his immense relief, no other vessels were anywhere in sight.

Midway through the previous afternoon, the ship's radio operator had intercepted the conventional British 'QQQ' signal indicating the presence of a suspicious vessel. A few minutes later, with the *Zamzam*'s radio men glued to their headsets, a second signal – a series of 'R's – broke in, followed by the message, 'Being chased by a German raider. Course due north. Fourteen knots.' The ship in question followed up by signalling her identity (Norwegian) and position – a distance of less than twenty miles to the south. Far too close for comfort. Captain Smith deserved to be well pleased with his decision to change his heading and put his ship well out of harm's way. But the presence of a German raider in the vicinity had been distinctly disquieting.[16]

Several days earlier, David Scherman had decided to embark on a photographer's marathon to record on 35 mm film the dawn-till-dusk activities aboard the *Zamzam*. His day began with photos of a holy mass being celebrated by French-Canadian Oblate priests and brothers of the American Order of the Sacred Heart. Next Scherman documented the Ambulance Corps being put through a close-order drill on the sun deck. Later on, it was evening vespers being observed by the Protestant missionaries, and his day's work was finished off by the light of a burgeoning moon with a number of shots of the ship's distinctive four-masted rigging and a few romantic silhouettes that he chanced to discover on the upper deck.

Three days and 28 films later, news of this epic photo shoot reached Captain Smith up on the bridge, and Scherman and

Murphy were issued an invitation to join the captain in his quarters for an evening drink. Their initial visit to the tiny cabin obviously provided Smith with a welcome opportunity for frank and open discussion, and he insisted on a repeat performance the following night. By all means, they must come along for another dollop of Drambuie.

As the commander of an incommunicative Egyptian crew heading blacked-out and defenceless towards South Africa's reef-strewn coast, Captain Smith was clearly a lonely man in an unenviable position. And Scherman and Murphy were only too pleased to provide him with the sort of kindred-spirit companionship he had been missing for far too long.[17]

On 16 April, Smith warned his passengers that they were only fourteen hundred and fifty miles from Cape Town and there might be rough seas ahead, but, with any luck, they should be docking within the next two or three days. It was time to start packing. Those who were especially impatient to put the voyage behind them immediately headed down into the hold and began retrieving their suitcases. The trip had been long, and Africa lay just over the horizon.

With new-found optimism, Olga Guttormson noted in her diary that many of the passengers had husbands and friends waiting for them in Cape Town. A beautiful young Canadian bride-to-be who was to be married within days of her arrival was among the most eager to disembark. Then there were the missionaries who had come to regard Africa as their second home; those who – like Olga – had been absent from the field for far too long and were restlessly waiting to continue where they had left off.

When Olga – a veteran of seven years in South Africa's mission fields who had been on home leave in rural Saskatchewan – first received word of the possibility of a passage aboard this long-awaited ship bound for Africa she was nothing short of ecstatic. In fact, just to be on the safe side, she had arrived in New York three days before the scheduled sailing date. After an enforced absence of two years from her cherished post in Natal, nothing could have pleased this dedicated soul more than the prospect of returning to the place where she would be able to continue the much-needed work she had begun there so long ago.[18]

Meanwhile, poor Kathleen had been forced to take to her bed, laid low by a mild but most unwelcome fever. She was, however, being kept up to date during periodic visits by her concerned friends Kitsi and Isabel. With the notable exception of the ship's Egyptian crew, the general mood was reported as being one of precaution tinged with a hint of apprehension.

> Mrs Lassetter had a 'hunch' at 1 a.m and had moved from her cabin to spend the night with another girl…(It was a hunch that most likely saved her life…and that of her precious Willy, as her cabin later took a direct hit)…Other people had gathered up their valuables, and others again had placed their life-belts by the sides of their beds. Only the Egyptians laughed at us. They just hid their heads in the sand, as usual, and assured us that the Zamzam was a 'holy' ship, and as the only ship which was automatically given right of way whenever she was in the Suez Canal, she could never be sunk.[19]

In less than twenty-four hours, the lives of everyone on board the Zamzam was destined to be irrevocably changed, but only a clairvoyant could possibly have foreseen the deadly threat that was lying in wait for the approach of dawn.

The surface raider *Atlantis*

Just beyond the horizon lay the *Atlantis* – also known throughout the South Atlantic as *Ship 16* of the German Kriegsmarine. She belonged to a fleet of nine such vessels that had been secretly built or refitted at the beginning of the war. In the guise of freighters, the intended purpose of these 'pirate' ships was to seize and – if necessary – sink any enemy merchant ships that were unlucky enough to be in the wrong place at the wrong time. As far back as World War I, the German raider's traditional function had been to seek out and destroy merchant shipping, as opposed to actively engaging or sinking enemy warships. To accomplish this, a raider relied almost entirely on the combined effects of stealth, subterfuge and disguise, but above all on the element of surprise.

Originally launched in Bremen by the Hansa Steamship Line as the freighter *Goldenfels*, it took only 14 weeks for the workers in the Bremen shipyards to convert the *Atlantis* into an armed and deadly threat to Allied shipping as Germany's first armed merchant cruiser of the war. The five-hundred-foot *Atlantis* was outfitted with a single Heinkel He-114B seaplane, four waterline torpedo tubes, and 92 mines. The ship was also equipped with six 150 mm guns, one 75 mm gun on the bow, two twin 37 mm guns and four 20 mm automatic cannons; all of these were hidden, mostly behind pivoting false deck or side structures. A fake crane and deckhouse on the aft section hid two of the 150 mm guns, while the other four were concealed by flaps in the vessel's side that were lowered when ready for action. At top speed the *Atlantis* was capable of close to 28 knots (32 m.p.h.) But perhaps her greatest advantage was her capacity to alter her identity through ingenious changes made to her appearance and all accomplished while the ship was at sea. Besides a dummy funnel, the length of the real funnel could be lengthened or shortened and the masts were telescopic – not unlike like the legs of a camera tripod. There was also an ample supply of flags, paint, canvas and building materials to achieve the desired alterations to the raider's appearance. In fact, with the deliberate aim of outwitting the pilots of any enemy reconnaissance aircraft that might pass overhead, the crew of the *Atlantis* was also kitted out with a variety of costumes, including white Japanese kimonos, round eye-glasses, and even a nurse's uniform complete with pram.

All told, a rather extraordinary ship, but no less exceptional than her commander, Captain Bernhard Rogge, who, in the post-war era rose to the rank of Vice-Admiral in the Navy of the Bundesrepublik and was widely regarded as an officer and a gentleman by friend and foe alike.

It was late August 1939 when Rogge received orders to interrupt a sailing exercise in the Baltic and return immediately to Kiel and then on to Bremen to take up his duties as commander of the auxiliary cruiser *Atlantis*. Rogge was instantly struck by the increased tension he observed at every turn, and concluded that his worst fears were about to be realised. The possibility of his beloved country becoming embroiled in yet another world conflict filled Bernhard Rogge with well-founded dread.

This devoutly religious son of a North German Lutheran pastor, who had enlisted in the Kaiser's navy at the age of 16 was one of the 1500 permitted to remain in the German Navy after the Versailles Treaty in 1919. In the intervening years, as a career officer, Rogge had rendered exemplary service to his country and at all times displayed the utmost devotion to his duties. With Germany now poised on the brink of war, here was a veteran officer whose impeccable credentials made him an obvious choice for an important role within the Kriegsmarine of Hitler's Third Reich.

Who – aside from Rogge himself – could possibly have imagined that there were serious impediments to a future that appeared so full of promise? As the Nazi Party's fanatical policies of racial purity were being implemented at every turn, Rogge found himself in an increasingly difficult position. Sooner or later, his Jewish ancestry on his grandmother's side was bound to create problems for him. He was effectively a second-class citizen of the Reich – a 'Mischling 2ten Grades'– and, as such, risked exposure and almost certain dismissal.

Nor were his concerns without ample and chilling foundation, for on his return to Germany from a South

American tour of duty early in 1939, Rogge was met with the tragic news that his adored Jewish wife and her mother had both chosen to take their own lives rather than continue to face the rampant antisemitic persecution they had been subjected to during his absence. Although there is no documented evidence of his personal reaction to this devastating revelation, it seems clear that the situation would have placed the burden of silence and sorrow squarely on his shoulders.[20]

Without the intervention of his old friend and Commander-in-Chief of Nazi Germany's Kriegsmarine, Admiral Erich Räder, the future course of Rogge's life could well have taken a distinct turn for the worse.[21] Räder, who was well aware of Rogge's delicate position, took it upon himself to request the Führer's personal dispensation, citing Rogge's long and distinguished record of loyal service to his country. Permission to continue in his present capacity as captain of the *Atlantis* was duly granted. Nor would there be any further discussion of Rogge's ancestry. It was quite simply a *fait accompli*. He had now been declared a citizen of the Third Reich whose racial purity would henceforth go unchallenged. Much to the chagrin of the Nazi Party bureaucrats who had been attempting to discredit him, Rogge had become untouchable.

Late March 1940 found the *Atlantis* heading out to sea flying a Norwegian flag, with an escort of two torpedo boats and fighter aircraft. After nightfall the ship was shadowed by a U-boat following a parallel course while the superstructure was altered in order for the auxiliary cruiser *Atlantis* to assume the first of her many new identities. In the course of the following year, *Ship 16* was destined to become the most successful raider of the German fleet.

By the time the *Atlantis* – passing herself off as the *Tamesis*, a Norwegian merchant ship, had her gun sights firmly fixed on the ill-fated *Zamzam* in April 1941, Rogge and his seasoned crew had been at sea for just over a year and were flush with the success of having seized or sunk more than a dozen ships, with another victim now within striking distance.

Attack at first light

When people find themselves caught up in a common disaster, no two recollections of the same event are identical. What has been a shared experience instantly becomes a series of flashbacks based on individual recollection, since the human capacity to remember is indisputably subject to personal interpretation. And while it is true that memory invariably assumes a life of its own, as an individual's powers of recall wax and wane, the mental pictures that are conjured up are subject to selective change. In reconstructing the tale of the sinking of the *Zamzam* these individual recollections come together to form a kind of collage of memories, placed side by side but always overlapping in time and space.

Thursday 17 April 1941. Isabel Guernsey had suddenly jerked awake in the early hours of the morning. Perhaps it was a combination of excitement and apprehension that prompted her to leave Kitsi deep in the arms of slumber and make her way out onto the deck. As she quietly dozed in her deck chair all hell was about to break loose.

Then it happened. Just about as suddenly and simply as that – at least from my point of view. Some others claimed to have had premonitions, doubts or fears. Not I – or I wouldn't have been out on deck in my deck-chair from the hour of three till six in the morning – especially as our Captain had told me that a raider's general practice was to follow up during the night and attack at dawn. I am inclined to think that that was exactly what happened in our case. That the 'something' that wakened me suddenly from a sound sleep at three in the morning was the subconsciously sensed approach of our impending doom…

The new dawn brought with it a perfect sunrise over the calm latitudes of the South Atlantic – but there must have been rain during the odd moments I dozed, for through the arc of a perfect rainbow came whizzing those awful shells, with a screeching tearing noise and a blinding flare of light. One volley had passed clear over us and another had hit the water short of us before I properly realised what was happening. Perhaps I wouldn't have realised it even then, had not one of the tobacco men who was also sleeping on deck that night sprung from his hammock and with a low growl of 'Christ, they're shelling us!' leapt past me on the run. That gave me impetus and I followed into the companionway which led to my cabin.

All was confusion inside. But there was surprisingly little panic among the passengers and almost no screaming, even from the children...Just a mad scurrying about of many shadowy forms in the blacked out semi-darkness...Even the three men, badly wounded by shell fragments or falling bits of ship's timber, were attended to quietly and without fuss.

From personal accounts gleaned afterwards, I don't believe anyone knew quite what to do. We acted on instinct, neither terribly afraid nor terribly brave; just dazed. I, for one, expected someone to tell me what to do next. No one did. So, with the shells still screaming over or against us at regular intervals, I made for my cabin, grabbed what I thought most essential and ran out onto the starboard deck.'[22]

In the cabin next to Isabel's, with the first explosion Kathleen Levitt was roused from a deep sleep to find Wendy and Peter in a state of unmitigated terror.

At first I thought we had run into a minefield, and rushed out to see what was going on. All I could see from the door were a few puffs of smoke which seemed to be coming from nowhere in particular, but just popping up all over the place on our starboard side. If I had taken the trouble to go and have a look at the port side, I would not have wondered for so long. A Nazi raider was shelling us without mercy at varying ranges...

By the time I returned to the cabin, having been unable to find anyone who could enlighten me as to what was happening and only seeing one or two frantic Egyptians rushing up and down the main staircase, I found that each explosion caused the ship to shake and shudder, and I began to wonder how long this old and much-used ship could stand it…Surely it could not go on forever…?

In spite of the fact that no alarm had been given and that no one had come to give us any instructions, I deemed it high time to don our lifebelts. All this must have taken place in a period of perhaps one minute, but it seemed like twenty to me. I found cardigans for the children, tried to collect myself sufficiently to remember all the other things which might be of value in a lifeboat, such as hats, which I could not find, glasses against the glare, a coat for warmth and something to eat.[23]

It was most likely at this point that Kathleen disposed of her incriminating passport – quite possibly even before she had begun to gather the children's things together. Her worst fears had suddenly become an urgent reality.

Up on the shattered bridge, after discovering that his Aldis signalling lamp had been smashed to pieces, Captain Smith was frantically flashing in Morse code to his attacker with an ordinary pocket flashlight, 'Neutral vessel – all stopped.' Realising that his position was untenable, he swung the Zamzam to broadside, indicating that he would neither run nor fight. The raider was now less than a mile away and still firing. (Months later, in magazines and newspapers throughout the United States, the Eveready flashlight company's enterprising marketers ran a gripping advertisement of this testimonial to their fine product accompanied by a purported quote from Captain Smith: 'Shells Screamed Our Doom on the Stricken Zamzam.')[24]

In total, only six shells out of an estimated fifty-five actually found their mark. One well-placed shot put the signal room on the bridge out of commission, making it impossible for the wounded operator to transmit an SOS. Another took out two lifeboats and a third struck the thin smokestack squarely on the much maligned 'MISR' lettering.

Before the next shell struck, sending splinters all over her cabin, Kathleen somehow managed to get the children into their lifejackets and was offering up a silent blessing for the lifeboat drills that had helped accustom them to these ungainly contraptions.

I must say, they behaved like lambs and Peter even helped to tie up the strings. I had just fixed the kiddies up and was reaching for my own lifebelt when a final shell hit the ship with terrific force sending shrapnel all over my cabin. The lights fell to the ground, glass splintering everywhere, the porthole was shattered and the inner wall came away from the side and swayed drunkenly at an angle of seventy degrees. Something hit both my feet, and for a moment I thought they would no longer hold me. Peter had been scratched by a splinter of wood from the wall and was screaming with fear and Wendy, although untouched was, of course, terrified.

I did not dare look at my feet but decided that at all costs we must get out of the cabin and find our lifeboat. Leaving everything behind, I hobbled out, dragging the two children and sat down on the deck on the side of the ship where boats were already being lowered. The terrified crew had made a mad rush for the boats and already people were descending ladders. Husbands were looking for wives, mothers for children, officers for their boat crews. The ship, by this time, was listing pretty badly and it was definitely decided that everyone should get into the boats.[25]

By the time the shelling had stopped, Captain Smith was already feverishly attempting to destroy any codes and papers which might be of value to the enemy. In his highly agitated state, he placed his British Admiralty orders under the blotter on his desk, possibly in the hope that they would be overlooked. To his chagrin, he would later discover that he had been sadly mistaken. He had unwittingly played directly into the waiting hands of his adversaries, and the consequences would come back to haunt him.

Meanwhile Kathleen's gallant Southern friend, Harry Cawthorne, who had promised to look out for her and the children if anything dire should occur, joined them on the deck and was instantly horrified by the sight of Kathleen's bloodied feet. In spite of her protests that she would be fine, he insisted that she must be attended to immediately, and dashed off to find help. At this point, David Scherman, his camera poised for action shots, arrived on the scene, and many weeks later, his photo of a woman lying helplessly on the deck appeared as part of a feature article in *Life* magazine.

In recalling her initial impressions of the attack and its aftermath, Kathleen's observations are an indication of her keen awareness of what was happening around her, in spite of her injury and the accompanying shock.

In an unexpected crisis like this people are liable to do the strangest things. Habit shows itself to be of importance...One mother, for instance, just before she got into the lifeboat gave her child to someone to hold while she returned to her cabin to turn out the light. And the father of a babe of five months risked his life to go back to his cabin to fetch the child's feeding bottles. Six young fellows (later identified as ambulance boys) had rushed up to the bar to save what they could from the wreck! And they did quite well, I'm told. It was twenty-four hours before they fully realised that they were now on a prison ship taking them to Europe and not to North Africa after all... (To their credit, the majority of the young Ambulance Corps fellows did their utmost to be of assistance with the wounded and were an enormous help when it came to loading the lifeboats.)

Two friends of mine picked up Peter and Wendy, who by this time had had a good look at the tiny little lifeboat bobbing about in the waves by the side of the comparatively huge *Zamzam* and had decided that it really was not a safe place and that they quite definitely wanted to stay where they were![26]

Tom Miller, one of the tobacco men firmly holding Peter under one arm, negotiated his way down a wildly swinging rope ladder and into the rocking lifeboat riding the waves below them. The moment Peter was safely deposited, David

Scherman immediately balanced him on his knee and continued taking photographs in rapid succession. When the raider appeared from behind the floundering *Zamzam*, in spite of the motion of the lifeboat as its bow plowed into the oncoming waves, David managed to get a perfect profile shot of what appeared to be an innocent black freighter, flying a Norwegian flag and bearing the name *Tamesis*. The raider *Atlantis* had been captured on film for posterity. Ironically, before the year was out, it was this photograph that would seal the fate of the *Atlantis* and her crew.

Scherman had instinctively realised that this vital roll of film must not under any circumstances be discovered by his captors. Using young Peter Levitt as a shield against possible detection by binoculars trained on the lifeboats, he hurriedly removed the film from his Rolleiflex and stashed it in a cardboard toothpaste box before jamming the roll of toothpaste back into its container and reloading his camera. As he later explains, Scherman's watch and – by force of habit – his tube of toothpaste had been among the few possessions he had selected as items that might potentially be useful in a lifeboat. Toothpaste of all things!

At the last minute, he had decided to leave behind his glasses, rationalising that they might prove an impediment if he should end up in the water. It was a last-minute decision that seemed to make sense at the time, but in the end its outcome became the source of constant frustration. Over the course of the next three months, without the benefit of his glasses Scherman's ability to see was seriously affected. Who could have imagined it would be the toothpaste that saved the day?[27]

Kathleen's account of her own dramatic exodus from the listing *Zamzam* vividly captures the sheer horror of those ten unforgettable minutes before the last shell was fired. To begin with, she had been quite badly injured by the shrapnel splinters that had lodged in her feet when her cabin was hit. Add to this the fact that she was still suffering from the effects of a debilitating fever and it is small wonder that she was slipping in and out of consciousness as the lifeboat slowly pulled within hailing distance of the *Atlantis*. Later, in one of her letters to her husband Lionel, she described what she was able to remember of her painful ordeal.

> I managed to descend the rope ladder, following two heavy American men and being followed by two more. We experienced a very bad moment when – with five of us climbing down at the same time – the old half-rotten rope holding up one side of the ladder creaked and half broke away with the strain.[28]

Along with Murphy and Scherman, there were about twenty-five in Kathleen's lifeboat when it pulled away from the side of the ship. One man was left halfway down the ladder and had to climb back up again, in spite of the fact that the boat was little more than half full. Fearful of the undertow in the event that the *Zamzam* might suddenly capsize, the men at the oars had pulled away furiously to propel the boat out of harm's way.

The contents of the boxes of food originally stowed in the bottom of the lifeboat had long since been picked clean and, not surprisingly, the blame was squarely placed on the crew. The bottom was littered with an assortment of poles, tools, empty boxes and bits of wood, but unlike two of the other boats which had turned turtle in the water, dumping a number of women and young children into the sea, their boat proved more or less seaworthy.

Mindful of his duty, the conscientious Egyptian quartermaster commanded everyone to remove their hats and turn them upside down in order to capture any possible drops of rain that could be used for drinking water. In her semi-conscious state, Kathleen was left desperately trying to work out the odds of being picked up against those of endlessly floating about for days before succumbing to a slow and lingering death from thirst and starvation. The sight of the *Atlantis* hovering only a mile in the distance distracted her from any further speculation.[29]

When the time came to draw alongside the raider, a large wicker basket was lowered, and Wendy and Peter were hauled up to the safety of the ship's deck. From below, their mother was watching helplessly with her heart in her mouth until they both disappeared from view, and that was the last she would see of either of her children for the next twenty-four hours.

In her recollections of her own ascent to the deck of the *Atlantis* she recalls coming to the realisation that she was unable to get out of the lifeboat unassisted because of the injuries to her feet.

> The quartermaster being by far the strongest and largest man in the boat tried to carry me on his back, and I can still remember the acute repulsion I felt as he gripped my arms around his fat, sweaty and very smelly neck! In any event, this method soon proved too painful and I persuaded them to let me haul myself up the rope ladder by my arms. This method was slower, but less painful and somehow I managed to climb high enough for them to drag me aboard. I was immediately carried into the Doctor's cabin and therefore missed the scene on deck...
>
> Peter and Wendy did not know what had happened to me and felt they must attach themselves to someone whom they knew would be kind to them.[30]

Taking Wendy's little hand, American missionary teacher Velura Kinnon assured the confused child that she would stay close to her no matter what happened, and for the next five weeks of their mutual captivity she remained true to her word. Almost two years later, Kathleen received a letter from Velura and her friend Esther Olsen back in America describing how they had found Peter standing alone and barefoot among the milling crowd on the deck. He was still in his blue pyjamas, spotted with tar and spattered with blood from his mother's wounds. When she approached him, he said something like, 'Miss Kinnon, I think my mother was going to cry. I think she thought she was going to die.' The kindly Miss Kinnon was able to assure him that his mother was receiving good care and that he needn't worry. Everything would be fine…[31]

Meanwhile, the occupants of other lifeboats trying to make their escape from the *Zamzam* had been having troubles of their own. Olga Guttormson's description remains a testament to her cool-headed attitude as the situation unfolded.

Orders were confused, and by the time I reached my assigned boat, it had already been lowered. I threw in my steamer rug and started to jump, but the boat was already moving away from the ship. I hurried to a second boat, already overcrowded, and was refused a place. Most of the passengers and crew had already left the ship, and the ropes holding the last lifeboat had already been released.

I jumped into the half-lowered boat, but the pulleys had jammed. For a moment we clung to the side of the sinking ship. Then someone located a hatchet on the floor of the lifeboat and began hacking at the ropes until we dropped into the water. The boat had been damaged by flying shrapnel, and quickly began filling up with water. We removed our shoes and started to bail, but the boat was overcrowded and the only possibility of keeping it afloat would be to lighten the load. We carried a number of children, so it became clear that the older members would have to get out. Tightening our lifebelts, we slipped over the side and into the water. The Atlantic was surprisingly warm.

By now most of the other lifeboats had already sunk. Some had been shot away in the early shelling. Others were badly riddled by shrapnel. The raider moved in close and in perfect English the captain was shouting orders through a loud hailer, directing those in charge of the lifeboats to row them over to the raider's port side.[32] Motor boats were launched to pick up those still floating in the water.[33]

Meanwhile, through the early-morning mist, some of the less fortunate, still bobbing about in their lifejackets, were vaguely able to make out what appeared to be a group of figures lining the railing of the *Atlantis*. As the raider drew closer, to their abject horror, they realised that what they had seen was a row of sailors standing with rifles poised for action and – worse still – the weapons were trained directly on the waterlogged survivors. But surely these men wouldn't contemplate shooting defenceless women and children? It was a terrifying sight. However, all in good time, the potential targets discovered that the sailors had been positioned at the railing as a precautionary measure.

On Captain Rogge's orders, they had been instructed to fire on any passing shark that should happen to appear. These noble intentions provided cold comfort to the poor souls who found themselves helplessly floating about on the surface like so many sitting ducks; however, the sight of the first *Atlantis* motor launch heading out through the chop to begin plucking people out of the sea brought with it a new glimmer of hope.

Among the first to be pulled from the water was Lillian Danielson, the wife of a Lutheran missionary from Kansas whose husband was already in Africa and eagerly awaiting the arrival of his family. Reliving the terror of finding herself and her six children huddled in a lifeboat that was rapidly filling with water, she wrote,

> Someone called for a bucket, but there was none. The men took off their shoes to try to scoop out the water and I volunteered my sun hat, but after much fruitless effort someone called out, 'It's no use. It's leaking like a sieve.' ... How insignificant we felt, riding the waves of the South Atlantic in a leaky lifeboat. As the water reached our knees it was time for action! I clutched little Lois, then 19 months old, in the crook of my left arm, then grabbed three-year-old Wilfred with my right. I asked my eldest boy Laurence, who was almost 11, to watch out for little Luella, who was then only four. Through tear-dimmed eyes I tried to smile assurance to Eleanor and Evelyn, one nine and the other seven, who were sitting opposite me. 'Keep praying in your hearts, my little ones. Jesus loves you,' I said as the

lifeboat sank beneath us and all thirty passengers spilled out into the ocean.

Our little ones soon bobbed up in their life jackets all around me. Our eldest son, faithful to his charge, pushed an Egyptian sailor off his little sister so she could bob up beside him. These were sobering moments. Our smallest ones were whimpering and spluttering as the salt water washed into their eyes and mouths, and I admonished them to keep their mouths closed and pray, telling them, 'Jesus loves you – yes, even more than Mother and Daddy.' The thought was comforting to me, also, as I was helpless to help them. I only had two arms. One clutched our youngest, and with the other I kept jerking our little son upright in the water, as his heavy lifejacket kept pulling his head backwards.

I didn't fear death for myself that morning...but I must confess I felt great pain within my heart for having brought our six little ones to this hour. Whenever a child was missing from view, I would anxiously call out. It was easy to imagine that the strings of a lifejacket had become untied and the little dear had slipped out of sight. No one can fathom the joy their voices brought me across the waves when they would answer, 'Mother, I'm here.'

The lifeboat also surfaced, bottom-side up. An Egyptian sailor climbed aboard, and Pastor Hult called to him, 'Reach down and pull some of these little children up there beside you,' which he did, and before long Louella, Wilfred and later Evelyn sat up there with him. I will not forget the sight of them shivering on the overturned lifeboat...I will also never forget the beautiful rainbow which arched over the whole sky in all its glory, reminding us of God's promises. By this time the Nazi raider had come to a stop a mile away and a motor launch was lowered to come to our rescue. The children were lifted on board first, then the women, and after that the men.[34]

Although the ship's passengers had acquitted themselves remarkably well in their escape from the floundering *Zamzam*, regrettably the same could not be said for many of her crew, who had been reduced to a state of frenzied panic. Some even resorted to jumping overboard in their wild anxiety to save themselves. And once they had been picked up and brought alongside the raider, to the utter dismay of their captors, like a swarm of drowning rats they struggled to be the first to clamber up the ropes that had been tossed over the side. The time-honoured rule of 'Women and children first' had quickly become 'Every man for himself and the Devil take the hindmost'.

Those who witnessed this shocking display of fear-induced cowardice could scarcely believe their eyes. Some of the horrified *Atlantis* crew members waiting to assist those clambering up the side of the ship actually had to resort to force by pitching a number of these panic-stricken wretches back into the sea. In their frustration, a few sailors were even provoked to the point of threatening to shoot any member of the *Zamzam*'s Egyptian crew who so much as touched a rope or ladder until all the ship's shell-shocked passengers were duly deposited on board the *Atlantis*.[35]

At this point, 36 people were still left on the *Zamzam*, including one wounded man and a little girl of four, who had been pushed to the back of the line when her lifeboat was being filled. By now, Captain Rogge had come to the alarming realisation that the ship he had mistakenly fired on was not the World War I troop ship that he initially identified with such certainty. Since the remaining passengers obviously posed no threat, he quickly dispatched the motor launches from the *Atlantis*. After picking up all those left struggling to keep their heads above water, the launches headed off towards the *Zamzam*. By this time she had somewhat righted herself and no longer appeared on the verge of turning turtle, which, in itself, was reassuring to those waiting to be rescued.

Captives

At long last the *Zamzam*'s crew and passengers were all assembled on the deck of the *Atlantis*. Most were in a state of dazed confusion. It had not been much more than an hour since the first shell had found its mark. The six Danielson children – still dripping wet after their dunking – were taken to a warm room below, rubbed down with towels and given dry clothing, before being tucked into bunks and covered with warm blankets. A few minutes later some chocolate cookies magically appeared.

Up on the deck, the crew of the *Zamzam* had been herded aft, and one of the ship's officers, using a stray passenger list that had somehow surfaced from somewhere, began taking roll call. To everyone's amazement, although there were four passengers who had been wounded, not a single life had been lost. Even Willy, Mrs Lassetter's infamous little dachshund, had come through unscathed and was making every attempt to befriend Ferry, Captain Rogge's black Scottish terrier. The missionaries were utterly convinced that their salvation was the result of a miracle that could only be attributed to the Lord and His wondrous rainbows. And even a few 'non-believers' were prepared to consider the possibility that an unseen hand had played a part in their rescue.

Once it had been established that everyone was accounted for, all the new arrivals were subjected to a thorough search of their personal effects: the contents of their pockets; wallets, money (with receipts provided), letters, passports, penknives, matches and whatever else they had been able to carry away with them. Snugly encased in its cardboard camouflage, David Scherman's film remained hidden in plain view. With great presence of mind, he had deposited the precious toothpaste carton into the top pocket of his pal Charlie Murphy's pyjamas. Both Murphy's hands had been bandaged because of the rope burns he sustained on his swift Tarzan-like descent from the deck of the *Zamzam* into a lifeboat and, by default, he became the most unlikely of all possible suspects. In the midst of the confusion on deck, the ever-resourceful Scherman also managed to conceal two additional rolls of film under Murphy's bulky bandages.[36] The ruse had worked like a charm, but on the other hand he had no idea what had happened to the dozens of rolls of film he had shot while on board the *Zamzam*. Had they been lost forever, or were they still stuffed somewhere in his hastily abandoned luggage?

Once the search of the passengers had been completed, they were further required to divulge their names, countries of origin, ages, addresses and next of kin. Then, after having gulped down some powdered limeade ladled out by a young German sailor in tropical white shorts, they were instructed to turn in their lifejackets and were sent into the fetid hold below. They were then led to a large area that had been fitted out with a hundred three-decker bunks for the purpose of warehousing prisoners awaiting transfer to a prison ship. It was here in this brimming sea of humanity that young Peter – still in his blue pyjamas and accompanied by the devoted Velura – was finally reunited with his little sister Wendy.

After enduring several hours of suffocating heat, everyone was finally summoned back up on deck to witness an unforgettable sight – the sinking of the *Zamzam*. It was just before two o'clock in the afternoon. The *Zamzam* was still afloat, and while the passengers had been left to their own devices below decks, the *Atlantis* motor launches had been running a non-stop shuttle between the two ships, gathering up whatever could be saved of the passengers' belongings – trunks, suitcases and clothing – to be hoisted and piled onto the deck of the *Atlantis*.

The foraging party had also removed mattresses, blankets, crockery, and whatever food they could find. Before setting the explosive charges that would send the *Zamzam* to her final rest, the scavengers had also loaded up on luxury items – everything from champagne and cigars to a generous supply of toilet paper, not to mention typewriters, radios, wind-up phonograph players and records featuring the latest American hits. Laden to the gunwales, the last of the motor launches to return to the *Atlantis* looked for all the world like a floating bazaar filled to overflowing with every imaginable treasure – even a child's tricycle and a few deck chairs had been tossed in at the last minute.

On his return from overseeing the work-party operation, Adjutant Ulrich Mohr, Rogge's second-in-command, reported on his impressions of the conditions he encountered while aboard the dilapidated old liner. The first words that came to mind were filth, filth and more filth, to say nothing of the wall-to-wall cockroaches and scuttling rats that had taken up residence in the ship's kitchen. In short, the state of affairs on board the liner was scandalous beyond imagination. In fact, Mohr could scarcely believe the passengers' remarkable fortitude in the face of the appalling conditions they had been subjected to for weeks on end. In his estimation, the faith and endurance they had demonstrated were exceptionally admirable.[37]

In an excerpt taken from the ship's log, a vivid description is provided of the scene of mass confusion on deck, as the passengers assembled to watch the Zamzam's last gasp.

Some of those who had come on board in their pyjamas were barefoot and wearing dressing gowns borrowed from German officers...Children were shrieking, crying or laughing. Mothers were wringing their hands...Babes in arms were peering mutely at the commotion around them. The children were highly delighted with this new adventure; the grown-ups were less enthusiastic. Most of them had lost many of their possessions. Some of them everything...

The ship's officers were besieged with questions from all sides:

'Where can I get some milk? It's time for Susie to have her milk.'

'Can you tell me where the sick-bay is? Perhaps I can find some diapers there.'

'Have you got lifejackets for all of us?'

'Can someone fetch my glasses and my manicure case? I left them all on the ship. Cabin 237.'

'Where shall we sleep tonight?'

'When do you think we can get off this ship?'

'I would like some iced orangeade … What! You haven't got any! How can I live without my orangeade … You're joking, Lieutenant. Be a good boy and tell me where I can get some.'

The officer looked at the woman straight in the eye and summoned up his best English.

'Listen,' he said, 'I no longer remember what an orange looks like or tastes like. On this ship we live on dried potatoes, dried onions and dried fish – fortunately not only on dry bread. The only wet thing, thank goodness, is the beer, and Dr Reil's whiskey and soda. [Reil was the chief medical officer of the *Atlantis*.]

'Oh, and do you think we Americans will also have to live on that (i.e. the rations described)?'

'I'm afraid so, yes.'

'And for a long time?'[38]

The same question was foremost in the mind of the ship's captain, Bernhard Rogge. Three hundred extra mouths to feed would soon have a drastic effect on his calculations of the raider's food stores, and he took great comfort in the knowledge that salvation was at hand in the form of their supply ship. The *Dresden* was hovering just below the horizon, and would soon be available to relieve him of this unwanted human baggage.

When the timed charges that Mohr's men had laid in the bowels of the *Zamzam* began to explode, the ragged chorus of cheers that rippled through the crowd of onlookers at the sight of their nemesis disappearing beneath the waves certainly struck a respondent chord with Adjutant Mohr and the members of the boarding party. They had been equally appalled by their brief experience aboard the once-proud old derelict.

Mohr, who had been a prominent chemist in pre-war Germany, was also fluent in a number of foreign languages. When he informed Scherman in fluent English that Captain

Rogge had given permission for him to shoot a roll of 35 mm film, Scherman was delighted. And Mohr, being a keen photographer himself, even gave advice about where Scherman should position himself, saying, 'I've found the best shot of sinkings is from here...Now, I suggest you get your own people in the foreground.' Mohr then proceeded to follow Scherman from one vantage point to the next, taking duplicate shots with his own Leica.[39]

The demise of the Zamzam was captured on film in its various stages, and Scherman later described it in his own words: 'Water fountains spurted up through her ventilators, her stack broke off where the shell had hit, and with a final tiny white geyser at the bow, she disappeared.' It was at this precise moment that Captain Smith was overheard muttering softly to his engineer, 'She took it gracefully, didn't she, Chief?'

Once the two photographers had taken their last shots, Mohr removed the film from Scherman's camera, labelled it and sent it up to the bridge, where Captain Rogge had already altered course and was on a southerly heading at speed, in order to be as far removed from the scene as possible. The following morning, much to Scherman's surprise, his roll of film was returned to him untouched.[40]

While all the passengers were on deck observing the spectacular sight of the Zamzam being put out of her misery, poor Kathleen was lying in the ship's hospital awaiting treatment for her feet while the three men who had sustained more serious injuries were undergoing surgery. One of these was the much-admired Ned Laughinghouse, the eldest of the Southern tobacco men, who had suffered a serious head wound from the first salvo. Ned's good humour and wit had been the mainstay of his fellow passengers in first class, and just days before the attack he had composed a poem to commemorate the shared experiences of their memorable voyage aboard the good ship Zamzam. The leader of the

British–American Ambulance contingent, Frank Vicovari, had also been badly injured in the leg, which required complex surgical procedures in order for it to be to saved. First-class passenger Dr Robert Starling's injuries were non-life-threatening, and recovery from his injuries now appeared to be more or less assured.

A number of qualified physicians had been assigned for duty on the *Atlantis*, so there was no shortage of capable and experienced personnel, and Kathleen, who had remained completely lucid while awaiting attention, later recalled her impressions of the hours she spent in the ship's hospital facilities.

The doctor's cabin was very comfortable, clean and attractive. A young man was putting it to rights when I was taken in. He had been given instructions to look after me and to bring me anything I needed, 'within reason', and in the future our needs were always to be very much 'within reason'. He was a pleasant-looking boy, about twenty-three years old, fair-haired, and with honest, well-set blue eyes. He spoke to me in pretty good English while he busied himself around the room hanging up pictures which must have been taken down during the time in which the ship went into action, winding up a clock, and generally tidying the place up.

He told me that a few years previously he had worked for three years in England in a factory in Birmingham and had liked it well enough…Suddenly he turned round to me, and in a quiet undertone asked me, 'Do you HATE the Germans?' This struck me as being a very awkward question to answer under the circumstance, but such an easy one to answer in ordinary times! 'Well,' I replied, 'I feel exactly the same way about the Germans as you feel about the English, I guess.' 'Yes,' he said, 'I suppose so,' and, sighing, he went on with his dusting.

For six hours I lay there on the doctor's couch vaguely wondering what they would do with us all and slowly getting over the shock of the morning's events. At about noon the surgeon came in, followed by three doctors, and told me they were going to operate on my feet. I was carried into the theatre, and noticed how very well it was equipped. In a few moments I was given an anaesthetic, and for two hours knew no more.

I must say that the Germans did their best for those of us who were wounded, but the others did not fare so well. Three hundred of them were put downstairs in a prison hold with instructions in English ('No Smoking') chalked up on the walls.[41]

As the light began to fade, the prisoners on deck were ordered to return to their communal bunk room and a request from the Captain was sent below. Captain Smith and one or two other representative captives were to join him in his cabin for further discussion. Charles Murphy was among them. Murphy's impressions of the Captain's quarters on the *Atlantis* were a far cry from Smith's spartan cabin aboard the *Zamzam*, where he and Scherman had enjoyed after-dinner drinks together on several occasions.

We were ushered into a beautiful little room with a handsome table, upholstered settee and gay chintz curtains. Rogge stood up and shook hands with us. He was a tall, strongly built, handsome man in his middle forties with wide-spaced eyes and beautiful manners. A full captain in the German Navy.

He apologised for the sinking and then outlined his justification – the fact that the *Zamzam* was running without lights, that the ship was maintaining radio silence, and that it was operating under British Admiralty orders. 'I'm sorry this had to happen,' said Rogge. 'I can only tell you that we shall do everything in our power to put you safely ashore, but you must remember that this is war and in travelling on the ocean, you have assumed many risks.'[42]

It was at this moment that Captain Smith realised the foolishness of his ill-advised decision to conceal the Admiralty orders under the blotter on his desk. Clearly, they had been discovered by the *Atlantis* raiding party. The liner's logbooks and code books he had long since committed to the deep, but not this crucial piece of evidence that had now worked so brilliantly in the Germans' favour.

To those present, it was equally obvious that Rogge was covered in embarrassment over the fact that he had just sunk an entire shipload of American citizens – women and children and missionaries into the bargain! Citizens of a country that Germany had been doing its utmost to pacify in the hope that it would – at least officially – keep out of the war. And now this! As a devout Lutheran, he was also greatly distressed at having captured so many members of his own faith.

In the wrong hands, Rogge was well aware that news of the *Zamzam's* fate and the capture of its passengers could well become a rallying cry for those Americans with an interest in promoting the cause of all-out war. Comparisons with the story of the sinking of the *Lusitania* in 1915 could easily be used to point to yet another blatant example of German belligerence. He would have to exercise the utmost diplomacy and caution with these Americans, and extend them every possible degree of courtesy and civility – most particularly given the fact that he was sipping champagne with one of America's most powerful and influential journalists. Damage control was clearly the order of the day. A hearty toast to the isolationists of America!

In the interests of good public relations, Rogge decided that it would be regarded as a magnanimous gesture if the golden chalice belonging to one particular group of missionaries were to be returned to them. The grateful recipients, who had left it behind in their desperate flight from the *Zamzam*, were overjoyed, and the news of its return quickly made the rounds. To Rogge, there seemed little doubt that – for the moment at least – the co-operation of his 'passengers' was virtually assured. And in any case, within the next twenty-four hours, Rogge's problems would be placed squarely in the lap of the captain of the *Dresden*.[43]

2

Prisoners of war on the high seas

18 April–20 May 1941

Aboard the MS *Dresden*

At some point during the night following the sinking of the *Zamzam*, the captain of the *Dresden* contacted Captain Rogge and confirmed that he was standing by to take the captives on board the following morning. The news of this impending transfer spread like wildfire among the passengers, as the approach of the *Dresden* had been the cause of much ringing of alarm bells. This, in turn, induced a mild state of panic among many of the helpless passengers in the hold. What could possibly be happening? All the lifejackets had been left up on the deck to dry out, and to compound their anxiety, the prisoners discovered that every last exit had been barred shut. Why would their captors be taking such dire precautionary measures? Despite a series of earnest assurances from the ship's doctor that there was really nothing to fear, the missionaries spent the remainder of the night in hopeful prayer, while the less religiously inclined passed the time engaging in nervous chatter or busied themselves playing cards.

The following morning, when everyone was finally permitted to come back up on deck, the prisoners were greeted by the sight of the *Atlantis* motor launches transferring their luggage to the *Dresden*, which was lying just astern. Captain Smith recognised her as one of the smaller ships in the North German Lloyd fleet which had formerly been on the Hamburg–South American run. For those waiting on board the *Atlantis*, the *Dresden*'s capacity to take on three hundred extra passengers quickly became the cause for renewed concern. With sleeping accommodation for only 35, the ship's captain, Walter Jäger, was facing a dilemma not unlike that of Noah with his overloaded ark. Having received his orders from on high, somehow Captain Jäger was going to have to find a way to cope with the addition of this unwanted extraneous human cargo.

Even before the boarding process got underway, the *Dresden*'s marines, kitted out in spotless white shorts, were already positioned with fixed bayonets to maintain a close watch over the new arrivals – as if any of this bewildered and shabby lot would have been capable of lifting so much as a finger in protest.

After sick call, which produced a spate of aches and pains as a result of the previous day's exertions, the captives prepared to take their leave of the *Atlantis*. With Adjutant Mohr acting as translator, Captain Rogge even posed for his picture with Captain Smith and conveyed his best wishes for the future. He also extended his formal regrets that duty had required him to sink Smith's ship... 'But being seamen,' he added, 'you and I understand each other. It is the politicians who have forced us into this position, and I know that if the situation were reversed, you'd have done the same.'[1] Almost certainly this was a point well taken.

One by one, the bedraggled *Zamzam* passengers and crew then filed down to the launching platform and clambered into the *Atlantis* motorboats, which began chugging over to the waiting *Dresden*. There was no sign yet of Kathleen Levitt, but Peter and Wendy were assured that their mother would definitely be joining them in due course. On the other hand, the three more severely injured passengers, Ned Laughinghouse, Frank Vicovari and Dr Starling, would have to remain under Dr Reil's care in the *Atlantis* sick bay.

At last, it was Kathleen's turn to be transferred, and she describes her ordeal with a certain bemused detachment.

To commence with, I was carried aboard in a water-proofed canvas ship's stretcher. I am inclined to think that one is always apt to get the worst impression of any vessel from a horizontal position! Being transferred from a German raider to a motor launch and from there to a so-called prison-ship trussed up like a chicken in a stretcher and knowing full well that a false step on the part of the sailors would mean a dainty meal for the sharks, was – to say the least – a novel and extremely unpleasant experience.

Therefore it was not without a feeling of relief that I eventually found myself lying on the floor still in the wretched stretcher feeling rather like a chrysalis, and just dying to free my arms. A few moments later the captain of the *Dresden* entered the cabin where I was lying on the floor, accompanied by the surgeon of the raider, and two naval officers. 'Where is the wounded man?' bellowed Captain Jäger, or at least I thought at that time he was bellowing but we were all soon to learn this was his normal way of speaking. I replied, with as much dignity as I could conjure up under the circumstances, that I was probably the person he was looking for. He looked down upon me with some surprise and grunted…Well what's to be done with her?…You know, of course, that accommodation on this ship is going to be very limited and that a cabin to herself is quite out of the question.

I could almost hear him thinking, Why can't these stupid English women stay at home instead of wandering round the world in wartime? However, the surgeon (Dr Reil), who was a senior officer, put him in his place by giving orders that I should be allowed to have one of the very few beds on board and that the two Greek nurses who were travelling with us should be allowed to sleep in the same cabin with me. After some palaver it was arranged that the two Greek nurses (C.T. 'Caty' Saliari and Parasaphino Poulu) and a Canadian lady (Isabel

Guernsey) should sleep on the floor, and that I should be allowed to have the bed…[2]

Isabel's recollection of dropping in to check on Kathleen just prior to the evacuation from the *Atlantis* is an indication of her finely-tuned sense of the ridiculous – a quality which would be put to extraordinarily good use in the weeks and months to come. As she entered the patient's room, Isabel discovered her friend, Kathleen, in the act of stuffing half a roll of toilet paper into her coat pocket. Without a word, Isabel promptly pocketed the other half. To have found seductive rose-pink toilet paper at the disposition of the totally male population on board the *Atlantis* struck both women as nothing short of hilarious. As Isabel noted, 'Another of life's amusing surprises. Germany must, indeed, be exceptionally well stocked with this particular commodity, if she was able to provide her raiders with such a fine-grade of tissue.'[3] Later, while aboard the *Dresden*, they were soon to discover that the standard issue of tissue bore a closer resemblance to sandpaper, and they regretted that they had not helped themselves to more of the luxury item while they had the chance.

Meanwhile, Wendy and Peter, still in the loving care of dear Miss Kinnon and her equally kind friend Esther Olsen, were directed to another cabin on the other side of the ship. While the men had been consigned to dingy partitioned quarters in the hold with crew on one side, passengers on the other, the 80 women and 34 children were crammed into relatively liveable accommodation.

A few – like Kathleen Levitt – had been allocated cabins, and the rest were relegated to the ship's 'lounge' on the upper deck. Kathleen's good friend Kitsi Strachan was among those forced to make the best of bedding down in this communal sleeping area with a lifejacket as a pillow. Her description suggests that she would have preferred to be more comfortably situated, but she was not in a position to register any complaints to the management.

Women and children were packed into accommodation for half that number. With twenty others I slept for thirty-four nights on half a mattress in what had been the smoking salon. As we crossed the Equator, the heat and the smell of that closely blacked-out room became almost unbearable…The food was such as one reads about, but never hopes to sample – unappetising watery mixtures, a flour porridge aptly dubbed 'billboard paste' for breakfast and 'glop', a thin soup with rice or macaroni base, with peas, potatoes and occasionally an unidentifiable piece of meat floating in it. Finding maggots was also a fairly common experience.[4]

For the children, on the other hand, provisions were eventually made for each of them to receive oranges from time to time, as well as tinned milk and a more edible sort of bread. Toothpaste and soap were scarce commodities, to be used sparingly, but, as the assembled throng soon discovered, the greatest inconvenience for the women and children above decks was that everyone was forced to line up for the use of two meagre bathrooms. Given that this arrangement was destined to continue for five tiresome weeks, at that point it was probably just as well that no one had the vaguest idea of the length of their extended stay aboard the *Dresden*. It would certainly have done little to boost their morale.

Another problem was the laundry, which had to be done in salt water, and from time to time Captain Jäger ordered the resident washerwomen to refrain from hanging it out. These restrictions were not issued without just cause, as the captain was undoubtedly concerned that the sight of women's underpinnings or nappies fluttering in the breeze might well prove to be a dead give-away to a passing vessel or aircraft.

Then there was the sorry plight of Elise Lassetter, whose beloved dachshund, Willy, was immediately removed to separate quarters. Captain Jäger had turned a deaf ear on her histrionic protestations and would not – under any circumstances – be persuaded to change his mind. He had quite enough on his plate without concerning himself unduly over the unreasonable demands of an irate captive…and a woman at that! Willy and his mistress would be permitted limited access to one another, just as the men in the hold would only be allotted brief 'visiting hours' with their wives and children and, on occasion, other female passengers.

Although barely twenty-four hours had passed since the *Zamzam* had been shot out from under them, for the most part people seemed to have recovered remarkably quickly and were now more concerned about waiting family and friends who would, of course, have no idea of their miraculous delivery from the Deep. There was a common sense of relief that their lives had been spared, and the women – united in their determination that the main objective would be to remain as healthy and cheerful as possible – made a point of insisting that the children behave accordingly. Whining and squabbling were not on the menu.

An excerpt from Isabel Guernsey's notebook provides a glimpse of these early days aboard the *Dresden*.

> Our cabin became known as the Night Club. And in it, nightly, gathered the ten or twelve less godly-minded, while the missionaries held their meetings in the dining-room or dormitories. As we were shut indoors at six o'clock every evening, with the ship blacked out and portholes closed and the lavatories not always working well, the air in any part of that cabin-class was positively stinking…The nights were awful. I normally do my best sleeping towards morning. Aboard the *Dresden* I was wide awake, holding my nose, trying not to breathe, long before the doors opened at six o'clock.[5]

But, in contrast to the lot of the two hundred men in the stifling hatches below, life for the women and children above could only be described as relatively comfortable. The men were subjected to the prospect of a bleak canvas-covered floor, two 200-watt naked light bulbs and the company of more than enough insect life to last a lifetime. And certainly there had been no preparations made for guests – welcome or otherwise.

The men were told that if they wanted bedding, they must fill up mattress ticking with some of the baled cotton the *Dresden* had just picked up in Sao Paolo. But, like prisoners the world over, they quickly discovered that shared confinement had the advantage of creating solidarity in the face of adversity. For better or worse, the *Zamzam's* crew and her passengers soon came to the realisation that, like it or not, they were all in this together.

Actually, it was a case of being *almost* together. A wooden partition had been constructed for the designated purpose of separating the whites from the non-whites. Rules for racial segregation applied at sea as well as on land.

In fact, almost the first of various altercations that the *Zamzam* passengers' chief spokesman, Charley Murphy, had with Captain Jäger came as a result of the fact that the Reverend Dosumu – a black preacher bound for Liberia – had been relegated by the ship's officers to the section set aside for men of colour. Nor had the good reverend registered any complaint. However, Murphy was adamant that Pastor Dosumu must return to the passenger section, albeit in the face of objections from certain Southern gentlemen, whose pro-segregation attitude did little to endear them to their fellow prisoners – the missionaries in particular. By the same token, the German Navy was certainly not alone in its policy of maintaining racial divisions. Its American and British counterparts also followed the same widespread practice of racial segregation, both in the ranks and among prisoners of war.

By consensus, it was agreed that Murphy would continue as the official spokesman and advocate in dealings with the captain, and would also share responsibility for a modicum of self-policing in handling the more fractious elements among the men facing a common ordeal. To make matters worse, there had been no indication of where the *Dresden* was headed, nor how long the male *Zamzam* survivors would have to endure these slave-ship conditions dressed in rags and tatters and eating what could easily have passed for pig swill.[6]

When Murphy returned from his first meeting on the bridge, he described how – in music-hall English – Captain Jäger had apologised for the inconvenience, but also explained in no uncertain terms that this could well be a long voyage and that it would be left to the men below to do whatever they could to make themselves comfortable. They must be made to understand that there was neither enough space nor enough food on board to fill three hundred extra mouths. Everyone must prepare themselves for the hardships ahead. And finally, their new captain made it abundantly clear that he was not in the least prepared to put up with any 'monkey-tricks'.

The next morning access to the baggage was permitted – priority being given to women with children. Rummaging through the mountain of unmarked baggage under the watchful eyes of a disagreeable purser proved to be a lengthy procedure. In fact, four days passed before the last man was finally given access to his possessions, but once everything had been claimed, those with more than they required wasted no time in divvying up the excess with those who had been left with only the clothes on their backs. Needless to say, all torches were immediately confiscated, and any alcohol that turned up was unceremoniously whisked away, since, in the captain's view, 'It could make for trouble.' All too true, but this was cold comfort when it came to parting with one's own private stash.

At least smoking was permitted, but – for safety's sake – only with due caution. In 1941, the joy of smoking was still very much a fact of life, and any interference with one's daily consumption regarded as a serious breach of personal liberty. For those deprived of the freedom to indulge in the pleasure of a cigarette whenever they felt like it, the sight and lingering scent of passing German sailors puffing away on one of the six hundred thousand American cigarettes that were part of the *Zamzam*'s remaining cache had roughly the same effect as rubbing salt into an open wound. This sorry state of affairs was only compounded by the fact that the prisoners had been allotted a single pack of raunchy Brazilian 'smokes' once every four days.

Hats, too, were as essential to the average male as his trousers. The Ambulance Corps boys and ship's officers wore their uniform caps as a matter of course, but there was hardly a civilian who had not left the *Zamzam* wearing a cap or fedora, and each had continued to wear it during every waking moment since. In essence, this simple mark of personal identity – not unlike the baseball cap phenomenon that evolved almost half a century later – was a powerfully symbolic manifestation of man's innate desire for freedom of expression. How something as apparently trivial as being allowed to sport one's headgear of choice could boost morale to quite this extent is anyone's guess, but the end result was nothing short of a universal truth.[7]

During these first days aboard the *Dresden*, the amateur navigators among the male 'guests' had been thwarted in their attempts to establish the ship's heading. At times it seemed to be drifting aimlessly with engines throttled back for hours on end. Then the helmsman would suddenly veer off in a new direction. This would be followed by another spell of heading nowhere in particular. Clearly they were marking time, but Captain Jäger was not about to divulge the reason for this exercise in dalliance. There were mutterings that the vessel was waiting to rendezvous with another ship, but then shipboard rumours are notoriously unreliable. The men came to the conclusion that it would make good sense to begin marking off the days on two calendars that had been nailed up in the hold. The prospects of a brief voyage were definitely beginning to look grim.

One bright spot in these days of endless dawdling was that Scherman discovered his missing Leica, which Adjutant Mohr had promised to return to him. David had long since given up all hope of ever seeing it again, when, quite by accident, he spied it sitting on a shelf up on the bridge, where – true to his word – Mohr had left it for him before returning to the *Atlantis*.

Afterwards, it also occurred to him that there was a slim but disturbing possibility that the rolls of films he had smuggled on board might be discovered, so he devised an ingenious plan of concealment designed to foil even the most intrusive search. That night, under cover of darkness, he carefully took out the two concealed rolls of 120 film he had originally hidden in Murphy's bandaged hands and poured some uncooked rice that he had cadged from the ship's cook into the central core of the film spools. The rice would serve to absorb any moisture, but to be on the safe side Scherman sealed the spools with some black industrial tape. The next step was to cut open the bottom of his Colgate toothpaste tube and squeeze out the contents into some mattress ticking. Following the same procedure with his tube of Palmolive shaving cream, he then stuffed the two film rolls into the tubes, re-crimped the bottoms and indulged in a self-satisfied smile. With any luck, the films would somehow find their way back to America. Certainly, taking these precautions could do no possible harm.

Phase two involved a more secure concealment of the 35 mm roll of film that included Scherman's shots of the actual sinking of the *Zamzam*, taken under Adjutant Mohr's supervision. The spool was re-inserted into its original hiding place – a roll of gauze bandage, resealed and placed in the medical bag of a fellow prisoner. The carton was labelled 'Antiseptic – Do Not Open', and Scherman could only hope that the German's well-established reputation for following rules would come into play, should the occasion arise.[8]

What the future had in store was anyone's guess, but uncertainty has a way of eliciting demands for answers and – after a good deal of earnest discussion – on the evening of 25

April – eight days after the sinking of the *Zamzam* – the men in their makeshift quarters below decks decided that the time had come to draft a formal petition on behalf of the neutral American passengers. This was duly typed out on a salvaged Underwood, ready for the signatures of all concerned.

As the immediate representatives of their government, their plea was addressed to both Captain Jäger and Captain Rogge, and it was earnestly requested that Captain Rogge's promise to the *Zamzam* prisoners while on board the *Atlantis* be duly honoured. He had given assurances at the time that all American citizens would be put ashore either at the nearest South American or neutral African port or, failing that, that they would be transferred at the first opportunity to a neutral ship. Among other things, the petition expressed concerns about the welfare of the five pregnant women on board and the nutrition of the children. But there was, of course, every possibility that these concerns would fall on deaf ears. Only time would tell.[9]

Through the British blockade

Then, on 28 April 1941, ten days after having so unceremoniously taken leave of her, the *Atlantis* magically reappeared. She had been stocking up on new supplies and fuel from another supply ship, and arrived carrying much-needed food for the malnourished Zamzamers, who had been left cooling their heels and growing increasingly desperate, their heads full of unanswered questions. Had the authorities been informed of their fate? How long must they wait to be released? What was to become of them, with food supplies aboard the Nazi prison ship running so perilously low?

It was a grey, rainy morning as Adjutant Mohr stepped briskly aboard the *Dresden* wearing the same ingratiating smile as when last seen, reported to the bridge to pay his respects, and then proceeded below for a visit to the men's self-styled 'home away from home'. Here he also passed on the news that friends and relatives of the badly injured men back on the *Atlantis* would be transported over to the raider to visit the wounded. This permission included the courageous wife of Dr Robert Starling, whose advancing age did nothing to deter her from descending hand over hand down a ladder with a rope bighted under her arms into the waiting motor launch below.

Meanwhile, no time was wasted in transporting a fresh batch of supplies from one ship to the other, and from their vantage point at deck level, the women were well positioned to observe the transfer, as case after case of food was hoisted on board along with a number of kapok life rafts.

Following Adjutant Mohr's lead, the *Atlantis* chief surgeon, Dr Reil, arrived for his own tour of inspection, and was impressed by the men's efforts at sanitation in the hold. He issued Scherman an invitation to return to the raider with him and join him in his comfortable quarters for a cigarette and a chat about yachting. Under the circumstances, the topic of conversation struck Scherman as incongruous in the extreme, but he was hardly in a position to refuse the invitation.

Once on board, permission was granted for him to take some photographs of his injured comrades. Frank Vicovari's leg was in traction and he was clearly in considerable pain. Dr Starling was faring reasonably well, but poor old Ned Laughinghouse's head injury had taken a serious toll. He was either asleep or unconscious. Prospects for his survival were hanging in the balance. A day later, the ship's log recorded that he had succumbed that same night at sundown and had been given a respectful burial at sea with full honours. For a variety of reasons – red tape and bureaucracy being among the most likely culprits – his many friends aboard the *Dresden* and his family in North Carolina learned nothing of his death for the better part of a year.

While Scherman was in the *Atlantis* sick-bay taking photos, Charley Murphy – with petition in hand – had entered into serious discussion with Adjutant Mohr and Captain Rogge in the captain's cabin. With Mohr acting as interpreter, Murphy spent a good hour stating the case for his American compatriots, and after a brief meeting with his officers, Rogge returned with a reassuring promise. His unspoken concern was that he had no idea whether or not this promise would be fulfilled. He informed Murphy that the *Dresden* would proceed northward that night, and head into the mid-Atlantic shipping lanes, where it would attempt to transfer the *Zamzam* passengers to a neutral ship. Failing that, Captain Jäger would approach the coast of Brazil, where they might possibly be taken on board a Brazilian coastal steamer, and if neither of these proposed courses of action met with success, the *Dresden* would then land the American prisoners at 'a truly neutral port' such as Las Palmas or Tenerife in the Canary Islands.

Mohr later recorded in his memoirs that in giving these assurances, Rogge was acutely aware of the possible political repercussions that the *Zamzam* incident could have on American public opinion. From past experience, however, he knew all too well that the poor wretches on board the *Dresden* were, in fact, completely at the mercy of the land-locked bureaucrats of the German High Command, whose interest in honouring promises made in good faith by maverick sea captains was next to non-existent. Mohr's outrage and frustration is readily apparent.

> Our promises were never kept! Only three or four days after the *Dresden* had left us we 'listened in' to a coded message from 'Higher Authority' – a code message overriding all our original instructions and ordering the *Dresden* to run for Occupied France. Rogge was extremely angry at this sudden switch in policy, feeling that his honour was compromised by reason of his earlier assurances. His views on the matter were subsequently

recorded in our Official Log and resulted in a severe reprimand for us both.

But whatever may be said about the military aspect of risking a supply ship such as the *Dresden* in a scheme to hand over prisoners to a neutral power, I believe, to this day, that it would have been far better had our original plan been implemented – even at the risk of the *Dresden*'s loss through capture or internment... We became the object of considerable contempt for having broken our word, although we regarded the plight of the *Zamzam*'s passengers with deep concern.[10]

Once all visitors had returned to the *Dresden*, the ship finally began to put on speed, and the resident navigation experts determined that their bearing was now due north. At long last, the waiting game was over. Their supplies had been somewhat replenished, and for a brief period the refugees of the *Zamzam* remained blissfully ignorant of the change of plans that the German Admiralty was about to convey to the ship's captain.

For the moment, the temperatures were still warm enough for the happy horde of children to be allowed to splash about in the ship's tiny swimming pool, and the adults were also allowed limited access. Segregation of the sexes was, of course, a given, and the *Zamzam*'s crew was also permitted exclusive access to the pool for their own private bathing pleasure. And all had been organised according to a pre-ordained schedule which Captain Jäger had magnanimously drawn up for the purpose. Undoubtedly his efforts to appear benevolent were all part and parcel of a desperate attempt to maintain friendly relations with his captives until he could be rid of them. Even at the best of times, this tactic could easily have become problematic, and as the weather grew increasingly brisk and the food supply dwindled, these attempts at a display of goodwill were all the more difficult to sustain. The mood among his unwanted fellow-travellers was approaching despair.

All hope of a release in Tenerife had long since been abandoned as the ship steamed steadily northward. To the few who were aware of developments in the North Atlantic, it was obvious that they were headed directly into the teeth of the British blockade. The Naval High Command in Berlin had remained resolute in its conviction that offloading the Americans onto a neutral ship would be putting the *Dresden* at considerable risk – a risk they were unprepared to take. Similarly, a stop in the Canary Islands was written off as potentially hazardous. The Admiralty's rationale was that the combined possibilities of the *Dresden* being followed or of the interception of her radio transmissions left only one possible alternative. The *Dresden* would make for a port on the south-west coast of Nazi-occupied France. There would be no further discussion.

If these instructions meant running the blockade, the decision-makers were convinced that this course of action still offered the best possibility for the safe return of the *Dresden* as well as its American passengers – who had so foolishly ignored the ever-present dangers of an ocean crossing in the midst of the Battle of the Atlantic.

On the other hand, the *Zamzam* episode had all the makings of a political hot potato, and from the German perspective all concerned had to be prepared to make every possible attempt at damage control. Diplomacy at the highest level would be called for – in full measure – if serious repercussions were to be averted. At all costs, every imaginable effort must be made to persuade US government officials that this regrettable incident had certainly not been intended as a belligerent act. In fact, quite the reverse. It had been a simple case of mistaken identity. A flurried exchange of telegrams and cables had already set the tempo of the diplomatic two-step. With any luck, the Americans could be persuaded to maintain their neutral position.

Back on board the *Dresden*, spirits were marginally raised by a rumour that within the next forty-eight hours the ship would be out of the danger zone. Had Captain Jäger actually managed successfully to thread his way undetected through the British blockade? As she suddenly veered off to the east towards the comparative safety of Spanish waters, it looked as if the *Zamzam* passengers' luck had held up against all odds.

The first sight of land on the evening of 18 May brought with it a communal sigh of relief on all sides – captain, crew and prisoners alike. The ever-stalwart Canadian missionary-nurse Olga Guttormson's account reveals a hopeful heart:

> This was the first glimpse of land we had seen since we left Brazil on April 10th. During the day of the 19th we idled off the Spanish coast and then drifted lazily into the Bay of Biscay. Tomorrow we would dock, but no one knew where.
>
> Towards midnight we speeded up and at 5.30 the next morning I went out on deck. The boat was keeping a steady course towards shore. Three German mine-sweepers preceded us into the port of St Jean de Luz, a former seaside resort and now a portion of Occupied France…Land and freedom lay just ahead![11]

The morning of 20 May dawned cold and grey. Saint-Jean-de-Luz had the appearance of a ghost town. The resort town's hotels, villas and rococo casino were looking distinctly bedraggled. If any of its inhabitants had survived the occupation, they were certainly nowhere to be seen. The Zamzamers did, however, catch a glimpse of a field-grey file of German soldiers emerging suddenly out of a waterfront barracks and marching slowly up a winding hill. In the harbour below, for the first time since her northward journey began, the *Dresden*'s swastika emblem was proudly displayed for the occasion.

The first part of the morning was spent in idle speculation. Nobody had been allowed off the ship, although a gaggle of German officials had come aboard and were closeted with Captain Jäger. People were standing about in restless groups, discussing what might or might not happen next. By mid-morning, a wild rumour had surfaced (possibly courtesy of a Swiss reporter who came on board with the German authorities) that only the Americans were to be released, but, for wishful thinkers, this was easily dismissed as a totally exaggerated possibility. How could it be otherwise?

By early afternoon, however, what had been written off just hours earlier as a wild rumour was now a full-blown reality. All Americans were to leave the ship at 1500 hours for transport to Biarritz, where a representative of the American consulate would meet them and arrange for their safe return to the United States. The other 28 women and children housed on the upper deck – Canadians, British and others who were citizens of so-called 'belligerent' nations were to remain in German custody. Full of new-found swagger, Captain Jäger informed them that they would be sailing on to Bordeaux. Having said that, he did hold out a glimmer of hope by mentioning that there was a proviso – probably thrown in for good measure as a token of his goodwill – that each case would be considered individually on arrival. Isabel Guernsey registered her own reaction to this news in her ever-present notebook.

> So, although our last hour with the Americans was packed full of farewells and messages to be delivered to families and friends, I remember feeling personally that some of us were rather over-dramatising the situation – that we would be seeing them all again within a week or two. This was just a temporary nuisance…The Germans were putting themselves to a lot of unnecessary trouble taking us up to Bordeaux only to have to send us back again.
>
> Still, it was a sad moment when the last small boat with the last of the departing Americans pushed off from the *Dresden*. A forlorn handful of left-overs, we lined the rail and watched

them go, our very good friends with whom we had shared an experience that binds people together in no ordinary way.[12]

Besides losing some good friends, we naturally had felt a sense of protection in the company of so many Americans. With their departure we waited with some interest to see if our treatment might alter in any way. After all, we were now the enemy, undiluted.[13]

Needless to say, those who were not permitted to disembark were happy on behalf of their American friends, who were now – at least nominally – free, but they were also hopeful that once the Americans were safely back on US soil, they would make every effort to publicise the fate of those who were still in enemy hands. What no one could possibly have known at the time was that on the day before the release of the Americans, the first news reports expressing concerns about the *Zamzam*'s failure to land in Cape Town had already broken. Quoting Egyptian sources, the *New York Times* announced that the ship was listed as missing, and the following day ran the headline, 'No Further Information On Sinking – No Official Confirmation of Ship's Loss'. In London, the *Daily Express*, in an article dated 19 May, was more specific, and voiced concerns over the possibility that the neutral Egyptian ship *Zamzam* might well have been sunk by a German raider in the South Atlantic. It also gave voice to one of Nazi Germany's greatest fears by making the most of the inevitable comparison to two previous disasters at sea with the headline, 'Largest American Death-toll Since the *Athenia* (1939) and the *Lusitania* (1915)'. and expressed the opinion that in the US public outrage would soon be heard around the world.

Another report read,

Certain New York dailies have come to regard this sinking as a clear warning to the United States on the part of the Germans that, in future, American ships carrying war materials to the Red Sea could well be threatened with similar action... It was further reported that if it could be firmly established that the *Zamzam* had been attacked without warning, this would be officially regarded as an act of piracy. At a press conference given last week, President Roosevelt also reminded journalists of the fact that the US had already taken military action against pirates on two previous occasions.

Given the tone of these and similar news reports, it is hardly surprising that diplomatic pressures were soon being brought to bear. On 20 May 1941, in an urgent communiqué to the Foreign Minister of the German Reich, the US ambassador in Berlin requested immediate information regarding the 142 American citizens who were listed as passengers aboard the *Zamzam*.

> It is obvious that there will be active interest on the part of the public and the government in the United States in the fate of these people and the Embassy ventures to express the hope that the Ministry will be in a position to inform it officially at an early date concerning the accuracy of reports about the safe arrival of these American citizens in France. Should these reports be substantially correct the Embassy will look forward to receiving from the Ministry full details concerning the welfare and whereabouts of the persons concerned and the plans of the Germans relative to them.

In response to this, on 21 May Germany's Foreign Ministry confirmed in writing that the American citizens in question had indeed just been landed at Saint Jean-de-Luz in German-occupied France. Upon receipt of this information, the American embassy followed up immediately with a telegram and a further request: 'Please make passenger list of these American citizens available as soon as possible in order to satisfy the American Ambassador's queries about the above situation.'[14]

Presumably, at this point the German officials in Biarritz had also received a directive from their superiors in Berlin to the effect that their 'American guests' in France were to be accorded every possible courtesy and consideration.

The Americans get lucky

Once in Biarritz, although their five weeks of Spartan living and severe food shortages had taken a significant toll, a jubilant mood prevailed among the Americans. In due course, the question of accommodation for the new arrivals was settled, and they were dispersed to four quaint little French hotels. The Germans, in spite of the directive from Berlin to treat their 'guests' hospitably, had taken the precaution of assigning guards, to be certain that no one made any false moves before their official release. Guards or no guards, according to Scherman's account, many a glass of good red French wine was quaffed before the celebrants finally called it a night and staggered off to the unaccustomed luxury of a real bed and their own private room.

The following day, 21 May, Henry S. Waterman, the US consul from Bordeaux, showed up and lost no time setting up shop in the Hotel Beau Séjour lounge with members of the Americans' designated committee to discuss the details of their imminent release. The group was later augmented by a German naval officer, a Gestapo man and two uniformed police officers who were in possession of everyone's passports and envelopes of money. Scherman had been a member of the small committee of passengers that had assembled in the hotel lounge, and his memoirs include the following description of his role in the return of the passengers' personal effects.

> They would show me a passport, I would give the name to an ambulance driver at the door and he'd shout it into the waiting mob. When the owner came in, I would identify him or her and he – or she – would be quizzed and passed along to the Vice-Consul (Coussens) and a stenographer who was compiling a list of names for transmission to Washington... Then came the money and the whole tedious process was repeated with the owners counting it and then signing receipts for what they got...

> There was an impressive moment when all the 'high command' gathered around Waterman as he dictated a historic cable to the State Department and – with the Gestapo man looking over his shoulder – signed it. Then everyone, clerks and all, posed for an equally historic picture before the Germans took off with a lot of clicking and heiling... That night our prelude to freedom was permission to walk to the end of our street, look at the beach and walk back.[15]

Before leaving Biarritz, there was also the matter of developing Scherman's 94 confiscated rolls of film for the German censors to inspect. This was easier said than done, as the local Wehrmacht had no photofinishing facilities of its own, and the first two shop owners Scherman approached were reluctant to take on the job. The third attempt proved successful. David and the German junior officer assigned to him were told they should return the following day, and Scherman could proceed with the work on his own.

That same afternoon, the American 'tourists' in Biarritz were given permission to leave their hotels for a few hours, and the majority seized upon this first taste of freedom to head off on an unexpected shopping spree. By evening, a number of them had returned laden with selected souvenirs, and some were already decked out in brand new Basque berets and capes to mark the occasion. Murphy, Scherman and company celebrated in style at a local cabaret, consuming liberal quantities of champagne and singing 'The Beer Barrel Polka' until the 11 p.m. curfew put a damper on the revelry.

The following morning Scherman and a couple of volunteers from the Ambulance Corps started in on the task of developing his rolls of film, and soon were standing in a virtual jungle of film strips that they'd strung up to dry on some hastily rigged clothes lines. Scherman had wisely concluded that it would be best to resist the temptation to pocket a few rolls because of the distinct likelihood that the Gestapo had taken an exact count of the number of rolls and would do so again. The films were duly returned to the German authorities; however, by dint of a remarkable coincidence, this was not going to be the last Scherman would see of them.

Many months later, the entire batch was discovered stashed in a shoebox in the press room of the State Department in Washington DC. Evidently, early in December 1941, an unidentified official at the German Foreign Office in Berlin had turned over the film to the US embassy just as the Americans were packing up to leave Germany in all possible haste. The United States was on the brink of war. All in good time, the contents of this much-travelled shoebox was returned to its rightful owner, and a second *Life* magazine photo story by Charles Murphy and his young sidekick David Scherman featured the long-lost photographs.[16]

Back in Biarritz, within a matter of days, the stranded *Zamzam* contingent in Biarritz received a visit from the American chargé d'affaires in Madrid, Duwayne Clark, and the repatriation process began in earnest. Clark set about the business of checking for missing passports, interviewing some of the more indignant former captives, making money-exchange arrangements and finding additional clothing for those in need.

Minutes before Clark was ready to head back across the Spanish border, Scherman and Murphy asked if he would take them for a quick drive around the block in his Chevy.

> When we got in, I said we had something special for him and without turning around he replied, 'I don't want to hear about it. Just drop it on the floor and I'll let you two out at the next corner.' Two rather beat-up tubes of toothpaste and shaving cream landed on the floor and we left.[17]

Before any further repatriation arrangements between Germany and the United States continued, a new bone of contention was thrown into the mix. The German representatives were unwilling to agree to the release of the ambulance drivers, on the grounds that as volunteer members of the British–American Ambulance Corps they must be regarded as belligerents and would, therefore, be interned for an indefinite period. As the five buses carrying their former shipmates pulled away, the ambulance boys were rounded up and ordered into the hotel dining room to await the Germans' next move.

En route to the Spanish border, Scherman's bus broke down at the foot of a steep hill, but there was much worse to come. When the party was turned over to the representative of the US government in Spain, Duwayne Clark surreptitiously handed Scherman a dirty brown envelope and told him to get it out of sight – and quickly! The tubes of toothpaste and shaving cream had been returned to sender. Now he was faced with the prospect of getting the package past the Spanish guards as they boarded the train for Madrid.

The next morning – Sunday, 1 June – when we reached the border, Franco's Guardia Civila got on wearing their square hats. It was the last terrifying moment. I had all my stolen film on me, so I stuffed the dilapidated toothpaste and shaving cream tubes into the outside pocket of my jacket. As the guard searched the bag in the next seat, I borrowed a toothbrush from Rhodie Olson and stuck it next to the tubes for camouflage. Then I walked through the train a few steps ahead of the guard and slipped Paul O'Neal the two bandage rolls containing the rest of the film to be put into his medicine kit. Sure enough my bags were chosen for inspection, but after two baby-dresses and a Hermès scarf, they gave up…Nearby a family of Jewish refugees were panic-stricken at the delay. When the train lurched forward across the border they laughed excitedly and jabbered in French and German. Their baby was the one who had cried all through the previous night.[18]

At the Portuguese border everyone transferred to yet another train, and two men from the American embassy arrived to provide them with an escort. Two days later the Zamzamers were safely in Lisbon. And almost immediately a cable arrived for Murphy and Scherman from their news desk in Manhattan, notifying them that their trip to Africa was cancelled. Within forty-eight hours Murphy had managed to procure two tickets for them on a Pan American Clipper to New York City via Bermuda. The consulate was briefed, and they were on their way. Or so it seemed.

To begin with the seas were too rough for the Clipper to take off, so their departure was delayed till the weather improved. The next day, they were airborne and landed in the Azores to refuel before setting off across the Atlantic. After sixteen hours of fighting strong headwinds, the Clipper reached the point of no return. In the interests of safety, the pilot announced that he would have to head back to Horta. There was no other choice.

Then came what appeared to be the last straw. Murphy and Scherman were bumped from their flight by three newly arrived US diplomats who invited them to join them for a drink while the aircraft refuelled yet again. It was at this point that Scherman was suddenly struck with the bright idea of passing the package containing the films to one of the diplomatic group – an affable Mr McAtee – with specific instructions to deliver it personally to Wilson Hicks, head of *Life* magazine's photo department. No one else would do!

The following day Murphy and Scherman were finally able to secure seats on a flight on an old S-42 Yankee Clipper bound for Bermuda and – as if on cue – one of the engines cut out an hour before they were due to land. But Fortune seemed to follow them in the wake of every potential disaster, and this was to be no exception. Once they had safely landed in Bermuda, Scherman was taken aside by a young British naval intelligence officer and ordered to hand over the films. Somehow the British had become aware of Scherman's clandestine stash and were desperate to lay their hands on it. With no small measure of self-satisfaction, Scherman responded that unfortunately he was no longer in possession of the goods, and that the 'loot' had already passed through Bermuda the day before in an American ambassador's diplomatic pouch. So sorry!

It was low tide in Flushing Bay as the S-42 rattled over LaGuardia Field and plopped into the Clipper base...Murphy and Scherman were the last ones off, swarmed by a barrage of old friends from the press and the newsreels. The next morning Scherman headed straight to *Life* magazine's head office and was instantly relieved at the sight of a pile of prints on the managing editor's desk. It had been a near thing, though. The person in the darkroom had developed Scherman's film for the normal amount of time and reported back that there was absolutely nothing visible. They were totally impossible to process. Should he just throw the entire lot into the trash-bin? As luck would have it, the woman who was in charge of the darkroom knew Scherman far too well to believe this could possibly be true. 'Leave them in the developer, Paul, and don't come out here until you have an image.' And, wonder of wonders, the 'lost' images gradually appeared. Because they had been taken in the half-light of dawn, the shots had simply been under-exposed. All was well, and they could now proceed to get the *Zamzam* story ready to go to press.[19]

One of the lead articles in *Life*'s 23 June 1941 issue, which appeared on news-stands throughout the United States was Charles J.V. Murphy's colourful account of the sinking of the *Zamzam*, accompanied by David Scherman's highly evocative photos. With a national readership of hundreds of thousands, the story was widely circulated and, not unexpectedly, it elicited a highly indignant public response. How could such an unthinkable incident possibly have occurred? Neutral American citizens taken captive on the high seas and held for weeks as prisoners of the Nazis...It was nothing short of an outrage!

3

Overland into the Third Reich

21 May–15 June 1941

Sorrowful farewells

Back in Biarritz, the mood of those left on board the *Dresden* was distinctly sombre. The last glimpse of their departing American friends had left everyone feeling bereft. Shortly before leaving the ship, the two devoted missionary teachers, Velura Kinnon and Esther Olsen had suggested to Kathleen Levitt that she consider the possibility of allowing them to assume temporary guardianship of Wendy and Peter in order to convey them safely back to America. But Kathleen, although deeply touched by their heartfelt concern, was determined that her little family would stick together, come what may.

> That afternoon, we departed northwards to Bordeaux escorted by two frigates. I was on the deck by myself, feeling sorry that so many of my friends had left. Suddenly, pandemonium broke loose. The frigates and the *Dresden* started firing machine gun bursts along the top of the water. The German crew angrily told me to get out of the way as they rolled what looked like barrels off the bow of the ship.[1] A few seconds later there was an underwater explosion, sufficient to noticeably lift the ship's bow. This happened three times and then all was quiet again. It seems the Germans thought they had sighted a British submarine.[2]

Beside Kathleen's matter-of-fact version of this briefly harrowing experience, Isabel Guernsey's description reflects her flair for making the most of a dramatic situation, 'We jumped, we paled, we shook in our shoes – and the German sailors laughed.'

Two days later, as the *Dresden* slowly proceeded into the Gironde estuary, she was joined by three more ships that had come out to give the blockade-runner a hero's welcome. These, along with the two accompanying frigates, formed an escort of five, which manoeuvred into a line-astern formation behind the *Dresden*. As each ship in turn overtook her and came abreast of the bridge, their crews hailed Captain Jäger and his officers assembled there to take the salute in what was regarded as a well-deserved tribute in honour of a magnificent feat. By successfully slipping through the British blockade, which was almost certainly a combination of blind luck and skilled seamanship on Walter Jäger's part – he had also brought his three hundred Allied prisoners into a safe harbour.

On the afternoon of 23 May, the *Dresden* nosed gently into the outer reaches of the port of Bordeaux and anchored for the night on the banks of the Garonne. Isabel notes,

> Here Captain Jäger was paid further homage. Several military and naval officials, including an Admiral, came aboard. Captain and crew were assembled, many Nazi salutes exchanged, the Captain's hand warmly shaken by the Admiral, and the crew addressed by the latter in a half-hour's speech, little of which we understood except that he was enjoining them to further effort for the Fatherland... The Admiral then made a tour of the ship and stopped, as he passed us by, to smile a bland, patronising smile – and welcome us grandiloquently to Germany.[3]

Since the prisoners had been informed that they would be staying on board until the following morning, the women and children made good use of the cabins that had been vacated by their American friends. Also, some of the men in the hold came up to occupy the area which had served as the women's dormitory and were able to spend their last night on the *Dresden* in relative comfort.

After 35 long days at sea, the captives were longing for the moment when they could at last set foot on dry land and perhaps even begin the process of negotiating for their release. As passengers on an unarmed neutral ship, their situation had all the makings of a reasonable case. What's more, they were all non-belligerents and the majority of them were either priests, women or children. Surely the responsible authorities would be persuaded to allow these innocent prisoners to return to Biarritz and secure their freedom along with the Americans? Isabel was not alone in her conviction that the transfer of all the non-US citizens to Bordeaux had simply been the result of botched bureaucracy.[4]

Early on the morning of 24 May, those remaining on board had packed together their meagre belongings and were already up on deck in a state of high anticipation. During what turned out to be an interminable wait – especially for the children – the Luftwaffe swooped down over the *Dresden* in a roaring airborne salute to the captain who had brought her home.

Finally the little vanguard of women and children received their instructions to disembark, trundling bags and belongings down the gangway and onto terra firma. How strange it felt, after five weeks at sea, to be walking on solid ground, but there was no altering the fact that they were standing in Nazi-occupied France. Still, they had been promised the chance of pleading their case, and this thought alone was enough to provide at least a vestige of hope. As for Captain Smith and the male passengers, along with the crew of the *Zamzam*, most were more realistic about what lay in store. Barring a miracle, it was highly doubtful that anything could possibly change the almost certain prospect of impending internment – most likely for the duration of the war.

For their part, the little group of 28 women and children had barely had time to adjust to the sensation of being on solid ground before they were marched off under heavy guard across some railway tracks, and left to stand forlornly by a line of dilapidated buses to await the arrival of the ship's men.

> When, at last all were locked safely into the buses, with an armed guard at the back and a French driver at the wheel, we set off towards town. After traveling about twenty minutes we realised that we were no longer being followed by the buses carrying the men. It was an odd feeling, for none of us knew whether we would ever set eyes on them again.[5]

The disappearance of the buses carrying the men was especially hard on the missionary wives, suddenly face-to-face with the realisation that from here on in, there was every indication that they were to be left completely on their own. After the many hardships these poor benighted women had already endured, the probability of an indefinite separation from their husbands was going to demand even larger quantities of faith and fortitude. Nor did the view from the bus provide much comfort. As Kathleen observed,

> It was Occupied France alright. Never have I seen such poverty and misery…The citizens looked tired out and half-starved. Many ships, nearly all of which looked as if they had been burned out or badly in need of a coat of paint, were lined up for miles on either side of the river flying a number of different flags including Vichy French and Nazi flags, along with Norwegian and Dutch, but most of them looked more or less useless. Guns were placed at intervals along the banks of the Garonne and I was interested to note that one or two factories had been gutted. Later on I inquired whether or not there had been any bad air raids and the reply was that every six weeks or so there was a raid, but no one took much notice of them.[6]

As the bus rattled through the city, there were countless signs of Bordeaux's last desperate stand: piles of sandbags, the rubble of bombed-out buildings and broken window panes, and the gaunt faces of the French refugees who had fled southward before the advancing German troops and were now reduced to begging for food in the streets. It was not a heartening sight. Isabel then recorded her impressions of what followed

> When our bus came to a stop, we all looked out and there confronting us was a large bleak building, with barred windows and faces peering out through the bars. This, of course, could not be our destination! ... Wrong as usual! Even when the guards opened the doors of the bus and themselves stepped out and waited, not one of us moved – not until we were told to. I shall never forget the look on our collective faces. It was grim.
>
> Inside the building, things took on a slightly better aspect. It was not a prison but a Red Cross shelter and the German Red Cross Sisters in attendance were not unpleasant, just wooden and mechanical, and so unbecomingly dressed! ... The first business was to divide us up – mothers and children were assigned to a large room on the ground floor, the unencumbered women went upstairs. As we traversed a long corridor to our upstairs dormitory, we saw through open doors some of those who had stared out through the bars on our arrival. These proved to be refugee families, mostly from northern France. Their stories would, I think, have been pathetic – as witnessed the small detail of a very handsome baby carriage in the yard below. I could picture one of these families, somewhere along the roads of France, fleeing the German invasion, their only salvaged possessions packed into that baby carriage. But on the whole they were a sullen lot. And in our eight days in this place, we made little progress with them since they and we were mutually forbidden to speak.[7]

For the most part, the accommodation in the shelter could have been worse. The rooms were relatively clean, the bedding on the cots was fresh, and the sheets, if coarse, seemed luxurious after five weeks of making do with an overcoat or a bare mattress. There was cold water in each room and hot if anyone wanted to haul it up from the storage tank of the stove which was kept burning most of the time in the yard below.

Bathroom arrangements, on the other hand, were another story entirely – even to the veterans of life aboard the *Dresden*. Only the valiant or those in dire need could bring themselves to venture forth into the yard to make use of the communal outhouse.

As for the food, after the ship's fare, the hostel's simple French cuisine was more than palatable. And the undisputed highlight of the week was the Sunday meal, complete with well-flavoured meatballs and two bottles of good red *vin de pays*. In the present scheme of things, there was little to complain about, aside from the disappointment of learning that the promised 'special hearing' with a representative of the American consulate was not about to materialise. Isabel reached the following conclusion:

> He had been forbidden contact, and one supposes that his position in the country at that time was so precarious that it was not wise for him to infringe regulations in any way. The American Consulate advanced each of us the equivalent of two pounds in French francs and that was all they could do for us…
>
> This was our second crushing blow. We had counted on everything being put right as soon as we could contact an American Consul. In fact, with every glass of liquid (wine, water or *ersatz* coffee) we drank during the next month or so, our toast was always, 'To the nearest American Consul.' This first one was so near but, alas, unattainable.[8]

To make matters worse, there were no indications of how much longer the *Zamzam* group would have to remain cloistered in the hostel. All thoughts of escape had been dampened by the consequences facing anyone apprehended in the attempt. They were to be shot on sight!

> We questioned the Hauptführer, but he knew nothing of our possible fate. After three days of this unblissful ignorance, of pacing endlessly up and down the bare ugly yard of that place, we could stand it no longer – and I conceived the idea of a petition, the first of many, to the German authorities… It was drawn up with considerable thought, and typed on a sheet of paper cut in half lengthwise (since someone had a typewriter, which had survived the rigors of shipwreck). The petition consisted of four points. The first asked for an interpreter. The second stated the last official word given us, that all women and children, regardless of nationality, were to be allowed to go free. (This phrase, worn

threadbare by our many subsequent petitions, became a *Zamzam* byword.) The third asked several weighty questions. And the fourth demanded, politely but firmly, to know why we were being treated as we were 'since such action seems unprecedented from what we know of German procedure heretofore.'[9]

The answer came within a week. On 28 May, the Zamzamers were back on the buses and headed for the railway station. Destination Hamburg.

While the group of women and children were left marking time in Bordeaux's Red Cross hostel, back in Biarritz, the 23 young members of the British–American Ambulance Corps were moved into another hotel and placed under house arrest by the German military police. Through no fault of their own, they had suddenly become useful pawns in an international game of diplomatic one-upmanship. The American government had begun stepping up its campaign of interning German nationals in the United States, and Germany, for its part, was only too pleased to use the boys in Biarritz as pawns in facilitating a prisoner exchange.

Within a month of their arrest, the prisoners were told to pack their bags. They would be boarding a train bound for Bordeaux, and from there to a more permanent German internment location. Not an inviting prospect at the best of times! Before boarding the train, two of them – Jim Stewart and Tom Greenhaugh – decided to make a run for it. At Poitiers – the second stop along the line, they dropped out of the train window, crossed the railway tracks without detection, jumped a wall and threaded their way through the blacked-out streets of the city until they found a trolley track leading out of town.

For a couple of nights they wandered the countryside across fields and through brambles and thorns, before deciding to take their chances on the nearest main road. Incredibly, they passed through an unguarded barrier without detection and within ten days were spirited out of Vichy France posing as two escaped Danish prisoners. After arriving safely in Madrid, they were suitably wined and dined by the US ambassador and given the news that three of their fellow ambulance men had also managed to escape successfully and were already in Lisbon.

As if timed for their arrival, an official letter from Breckenridge Long – the US Assistant Secretary of State – landed on the ambassador's desk informing him that 'The German Government has agreed to the release of the American members of the British–American Ambulance Corps, who had been taken off the steamship, *Zamzam* by a German raider and detained by the German authorities in Occupied France.'[10] In the end, the escapees' flight to freedom had bought them precisely nothing.

On 14 July, three arduous months after their capture at sea, Stewart and Greenhaugh joined their Ambulance Corps pals in Lisbon and – with the exception of their badly injured leader, Frank Vicovari, who was still aboard the *Atlantis* – the entire contingent sailed for America on the *West Point*, the same ship that had transported the German internees from the United States in the other direction.

As to the fate of their less fortunate friends in Occupied France – those who still remained in enemy hands – the situation was looking bleaker by the day. While boarding the very long prison-train that would carry them northward into the Third Reich, the women and children – fresh from the Red Cross hostel – briefly caught sight of the male *Zamzam* prisoners on the platform of Bordeaux station. No one was missing – not even the Italian prince who had been quite sure, the last night on the *Dresden*, that his case would receive special consideration in Bordeaux. They were all there! The fact that everyone was on the same train brought at least a small measure of comfort in an otherwise dire situation.

While the full complement of male prisoners of war – at least four hundred of them taken from seven or eight different vessels – were packed into what amounted to cattle cars at the rear, the women and children were crammed into compartments fitted out with hard wooden benches, where it was next to impossible for anyone to stretch their legs unless they received permission to walk the narrow corridor that led to the WC. Food consisted of bread and tinned horse meat, but as they travelled through France, they encountered a totally unexpected degree of generosity on the part of the local population. It was an experience that Olga Guttormson would never forget.

> At our last French stop, a man hurried back and forth to a nearby well to secure water for as many of us as possible. Another handed us a long sausage with greetings from the butcher…Just as the train was pulling out, a man came running with a loaf of bread from the baker and handed it through our window. The soul of France was still free.[11]

After the train crossed the German border at Strasbourg, it continued north for several more days, passing through the Saar Valley and onward to the Hannover region before turning towards Bremerhaven and the North Sea coast. Once in Hamburg, all the male prisoners – including Captain Smith and the husbands of the *Zamzam* women – would set off on a long march to Sandbostel, a POW camp which the Nazis had designated for the internment of captured sailors of the merchant navy.[12] (Sandbostel, as well as Stalag XB, were the prison camps in north-west Germany where the crew and other male prisoners from the *Zamzam* [including 17 French-Canadian missionary priests who later served as chaplains] were interned. The combined camps covered 1.5 km² and had been built to house twenty-five thousand prisoners. Some of the priests and civilian prisoners were later sent to other camps.)

Vida Steele, the Canadian missionary, whose husband had been among the men imprisoned in the tail end of the same train, later described the journey and its aftermath.

> It took six or seven days and nights to travel to Hamburg, because if there was an important train coming through, we were put on a side track. During this time, I would put my head out the window and if one of the men were looking, they would notify my

husband and we could wave to each other…When we arrived in Hamburg, the husbands were given two minutes to say good-bye to their wives. It was a sad parting![13]

After enduring the cramped and uncomfortable journey on the prison train, this was the last time that Vida would see her husband, Ellsworth, for many months to come. When they waved good-bye to their home and children in Three Hills, Alberta, almost ten weeks earlier to take up a post in the Belgian Congo, their decision had been based on the advice of their mission. It was considered the better part of wisdom for the Steeles to leave their two children, aged nine and twelve, with relatives in Canada until after the war's end in case of misadventure during the ocean crossing.

Ironically, Ellsworth had been born in the United States, and after moving to Canada held dual citizenship. Upon hearing through the gospel grapevine that it was easier for Canadians to get assigned to missions in Africa, Ellsworth decided to apply for a Canadian passport just a matter of months before he and Vida set sail from New York Harbour aboard the *Zamzam*. Had he retained his US passport, both of them would have been released with the other Americans in Biarritz. But clearly this was not meant to be.

For the small group of *Zamzam* women and children – English, Canadians and South Africans, a woman from Cyprus, another from France as well as one Norwegian – the Germans had other plans, although at times it appeared as if they were being formulated by guess and by God. In a letter written by Kathleen to her husband in South Africa several weeks after she and the children were eventually settled in a long-term internment facility, she was able to recall vividly the details of their journey through the Third Reich, including the dramatic arrival in Hamburg.

There was great excitement on the platform as many German naval officers had come to meet the prison train to point and gawk at us, and to take cinephotos of 'the catch'. I am afraid we did not give them much satisfaction as almost everyone turned their backs on the cameras – even the children…[14]

She went on to describe the pervasive feeling of helplessness that everyone experienced as they watched the male prisoners being marched away.[15] On the other hand, no one was given much time to dwell on this, as an English-speaking naval officer approached them almost immediately. Isabel called him the Admiral – though he may well have held a somewhat less elevated rank – because of his general charm and the dignity of his bearing. He informed them that their arrival had not been expected, that he regretted he had no proper accommodation to offer them, that temporary provision was being made which he feared was less comfortable than he might have wished for, but in a few days' time they would begin their journey to an internment camp in the south of Germany and there everything would be most pleasant. He then directed the older women and the mothers and children to a waiting bus, and escorted the rest of the group to the garden of a nearby hotel, where he suggested that everyone should sit and have some lemonade as his guests while waiting for transport to their accommodation.[16] Somehow, though, in spite of his attempts at gallantry, his parting words, 'You have nothing to worry about!', lacked the genuine ring of reassurance.

Jail-hopping

From Hamburg, a prison van transported its occupants to Wesermünde, a smaller town which lay about an hour's ride to the south, in the vicinity of Bremerhaven. Kathleen's recollection of their accommodation in this place leaves little to the imagination:

As we approached our destination, I looked anxiously out the window for signs of a comfortable hotel, but could see no sign of anything. We slowed down and the Gestapo man jumped out, went to the door of a building and rang the bell. I shall never forget the sound of that bell – it was ominous to say the least and jangled through the stone walls…After a moment or two the door was opened by a most unfriendly-looking policeman with a huge bunch of keys dangling from his wrist.

He shook hands with the Gestapo fellow and then began yelling at us to get down from the vehicle and lug our baggage into the hall. This was not such an easy matter, but we helped each other along and after much shouting by our overseer and a lot of pulling and tugging, we managed to bring it all in…When we had first seen this man coming out to meet us, what we had not bargained for was that we were actually about to be subjected to sixteen days in a series of German prisons. We immediately informed the fellow in charge that we felt there had been some mistake. We were civil internees, not criminals and surely this was against international law…[17]

In reply, the Herr Inspektor merely laughed and informed the ladies that Germany had neither the time nor the inclination to worry about an insignificant group of women and children; that this was one of the best prisons in the Reich and they were extremely lucky to be there. If they behaved themselves, he had no doubt that everything would resolve itself accordingly.

The Levitt family – Kathleen, Wendy and Peter – were told that they had been fortunate enough to be allotted a private cell. They were led up some stairs and into a cupboard-sized space with two beds strapped to the walls, a table and stool and a small grated window set high in the stone wall. The door was noisily slammed behind them, then locked and barred. Wendy began to wail and Peter was less than enthusiastic. Eventually Kathleen managed to divert the children's attention by telling them a story, but she had scarcely begun when Herr Inspektor Baum came in to ask why the little girl was crying. Were they not happy? Kathleen was reluctant to offer a suitably candid answer, but as one day unfolded into the next, their jailer seemed inclined to believe that his prisoners clearly did not pose a serious threat to Nazi Germany and could be given greater consideration.

One evening when I went up to my 'private' cell, I was surprised to find the door open and the light on. I had settled the children in bed two hours previously and they were always so exhausted that they fell asleep immediately. I walked in and found an aged gaoler, with a long white beard gently caressing Wendy on the head with his hand. He was slightly drunk but in a harmless mood. 'How sweet,' he was saying, 'but fancy putting a little child in prison. This is no place for her.' I was inclined to agree with him, but neither he nor I had any influence to do much about it…

As the children, by this time, were really looking pretty bad, I thought I would try and see if the doctor could help us at all. I lied to the man in charge and said that my child was really very ill and that I must see a doctor at once. He sympathised and promised to arrange for us to pay the prison doctor a visit. Then came our first introduction to a Black Maria. We were bundled into one, whirled through space, and deposited outside a huge building crammed with Gestapo, and police offices.

We climbed to the top floor and waited outside an office for about three quarters of an hour for His Lordship. The Doctor was an enormous man, more like a butcher than a medical man and I should say with about as much sympathy for his patients. He looked at Wendy, shook his head and said, 'Yes, I can see a serious case of rickets! Must have had it for years, lots of children have it these days.' This was really marvellous, the child was supposed to be suffering from a disease I was quite certain she did not have, nor ever had had! Now what was he going to do about it?

What he did was not much, but it helped a bit and enabled me to go shopping in the town and have a good look round. He ordered that Wendy should have cod liver oil and should be released from the prison during the daytime and be allowed out in the sunshine. As she was out in the yard all day the authorities did not allow her outside the gates, but Herr Inspector Baum did take me shopping with him – the first of five expeditions I was to make in the town.

In the evenings it was our habit to sit outside in the yard, until the very last moment; and one occasion we were partaking of our tasty black bread and fat when four rather good-looking young officers sat themselves on the sill of one of the windows to the right of us and tried to make themselves as pleasant as possible. They put their wireless set on the sill, and allowed us to listen to *The Tales of Hoffmann*, which we all enjoyed; then, to our amazement, they threw us down three packets of knackerbrot, a sort of crisp biscuit, which is very tasty, and half a white roll each. Then alas, they thought they would render us another kindness. They tuned in to Lord Haw Haw! They were simply astounded when we just howled with laughter at all the really terrible news he was passing over to the English – or trying to…It's true, they shouted, Why do you laugh? But we knew…and anyway even if there was a grain of truth in what he was saying, we were not going to let them see that it worried us.

'Lord Haw-Haw' was the nickname of William Joyce, an Irishman, whose radio programme *Germany Calling* was broadcast from 1939 to 1945. As a known pre-war Fascist in Britain, Joyce had fled England and almost instantly become a committed citizen of Hitler's Third Reich. *Germany Calling* was aimed at listeners in England who might be deluded enough to believe the propaganda that Joyce offered the world from Bremen. Due to his distinctively nasal voice and sarcastic tone, his broadcasts acquired a widely recognised reputation and became the object of national derision in Britain as purveyors of lies.

> I cannot with truth say that any of us were sorry to leave the jail at Wesermünde in spite of the fact that we had often been assured that it was one of the most comfortable ones in Germany. We really could not believe that one, but we were soon to learn that this particular tale was true.[18]

After nine days of less-than-five-star accommodation in the Wesermünde jail, the prisoners' next stop was an overnight stay in the Reich's Hannover facilities, where the entire party was locked in a single cell and confined there for thirty-six hours. They slept side-by-side on a sort of raised platform that doubled as a bed, covered with straw-filled sacking. To their chagrin, the following morning they discovered that virtually no one had escaped being bitten by the local insect population, which was very much alive and well-fed. To make matters worse, the insistent shrieking of the air-raid sirens and the low drone of aircraft overhead had prevented almost everyone but the children from getting much sleep.

By the time the party of 28 left Hannover, almost two full months had elapsed since the sinking of the *Zamzam*; however, their jail-time as guests of the Third Reich was fast drawing to a close. Stuttgart would be the last stop before they reached their final destination near Germany's south-western border with Switzerland. Isabel's impressions were duly recorded in her notebook:

> From trains to jails and vice versa we were escorted by cordons of police. And I didn't wonder that on-lookers at the stations gaped as this comic opera scene of twenty-eight women and children with at least one policeman to each one of us. Our dress alone was enough to stir anyone's curiosity. For instance, my friend with the crushed feet [Kathleen], who still couldn't get into regular shoes and toured the jails in dirty-white running-shoes and a mink coat saved from the shipwreck. But again I must say that Germans are kind to children, and at almost every station the youngest children were carried from train to Black Maria in the arms of the police. And I firmly believe that it was because we had small children with us that our journey to the internment camp was eventually cut short by at least several jails. So that from Hannover to Stuttgart and from the latter to Meckenbeuren (the village closest to our Liebenau camp), we accomplished the considerable distance in one-day hops.
>
> Stuttgart jail was interesting by virtue of several sidelights. It housed, besides us, many French political prisoners, who never saw the light of day, and who whispered to us, asking for cigarettes, through the ventilators of their dark cells when we were allowed out into the corridor to wash or exercise. Further, the South German police were noticeably nicer than their northern counterparts in Bremen and Hannover – softer in voice, more gentle in manner – even apologetic for the Gestapo's crudeness.

A plain-clothes Gestapo official visited us during the course of the one long day we spent in Stuttgart. He entered our cell without any warning. His entry claimed all our attention, naturally – but, also naturally, we remained seated. He barked out: 'Stehen Sie auf,' in a voice that brooked no refusal – and those who didn't understand followed suit in standing up with those who did. And it is perhaps interesting to remark that our gaoler, who accompanied the Gestapo man, returned later to offer a semi-apology or explanation of this intrusion: it was part of the regular Sunday inspection tour, and this official hadn't properly understood who or what we were![19]

The group had been allocated two adjoining rooms, and everyone was pleasantly surprised to find that – miracle of miracles – they'd been given clean sheets and mattresses. Outside the rooms was a large and airy corridor with a stone floor, where they were obliged to take exercise three times a day, and they could also wash themselves at the two cold-water taps at the end of the hall. To help pass the time, one of the younger women decided it might be fun to initiate everyone into the latest dance craze – the 'palais glide' – and many giddy hours were spent prancing up and down the length of the hallway. This bit of frivolity must have inspired the *Zamzam*'s fun-loving Greek stewardess to offer to tell people's fortunes, which helped to keep everyone entertained later that night. By the glow of a flashlight, they sat in a ring around her on the bare prison floor as she told each person's fortune. Given the surroundings, it was an incongruous pastime, but it helped serve the purpose of lifting everyone's spirits during this brief stopover while under lock and key in Stuttgart.

The journey from Stuttgart to Meckenbeuren was the last lap of our journey and the best. Again we travelled by second-class coach instead of prison wagon. We felt we were at last arriving somewhere, even though we had no clear idea of the character of our destination. We were anxious to arrive there, no matter what. And perhaps our guards felt they would soon be freed of an unwanted responsibility, for they gave us considerable liberty on the train and at Ulm, they even allowed us to buy biscuits and beer.[20]

4

Liebenau internment camp
16 June–13 September 1941

The many faces of a new-found paradise

The arrival at Liebenau of the group of 28 women and children coincided almost two months to the day with the sinking of the *Zamzam* and the beginning of life as prisoners of war. It might just as well have been an eternity! After their harrowing pillar-to-post odyssey by train from Bordeaux, zigzagging through the length of Germany to the North Sea and then all the way back to its southernmost boundary with Switzerland, they had almost become accustomed to the gypsy-like routine that had been forced upon them. Before Liebenau, this process of continual chopping and changing had gradually begun to evolve into a strange new existence, in which the beginning of each day could well mean another round of packing up and moving on to the next place of confinement.

It also remained something of a mystery that wherever they went they were always accompanied by a disproportionate number of armed guards. Peter Levitt's six-year-old mind simply failed to fathom why the Germans found it necessary to go to such extraordinary lengths to keep a group of women and children under virtually constant surveillance. Certainly, his mother was at a loss to explain it, except to say that this was simply the way things were done in Germany and – like it or not – they must make the best of it.[1]

The prisoners arrived by train from nearby Meckenbeuren at three o'clock in the afternoon, and were met at the station by the camp car and a horse-drawn cart which would transport the mothers and smallest children along with the baggage, while the rest of the group made the 4km trek in the gently falling spring rain through the sheltering forests and hilly farmland that surrounded the camp. Within the hour they were greeted with the sight of what would become their new home away from for some time to come – the cloister of Liebenau.

Isabel's reaction to her first glimpse of Liebenau recaptures the sense of almost overwhelming relief that sent everyone's spirits soaring:

> I shall never forget our arrival there. The Convent buildings stood bathed in late afternoon sunlight – the soft kind of sunlight that comes after rain. The flower beds around the children's pool were a mass of sweet old-fashioned bloom – pinks, pansies and those small English daisies that look for all the world like rosy chubby children. And people spoke our own language and were kind to us. There were Red Cross parcels with chocolate and Canadian butter, and cigarettes. I had my first decent bath in months and a clean bed and somebody even gave me a new nightie. After the filth and misery we had been through, it was almost too much.[2]

Kitsi Strachan would later write her own first impressions of Liebenau's story-book setting:

> Quiet Liebenau after those strange bewildering weeks when our world seemed to have turned completely upside down was – in comparison – a real haven of rest and comfort. The camp was situated in beautiful rolling countryside interspersed with quaint villages. Twenty miles to the south across Lake Constance, on fine days the Swiss Alps would emerge from behind the clouds like the magical mountains of a fairy tale and then just as silently disappear again…There were two modern buildings – Josefshaus, where I lived, and Clarahaus, but far more picturesque was the Schloss, dating back to 1570 with its steep grey walls

and turreted roofs. Between the buildings were lovely stretches of lawn and shrubbery edged by flowerbeds, carefully tended by the nuns.[3]

To these much-travelled women and children, Liebenau gave the impression of being a place where they would be free to see and do things that had been unimaginable during their two long months of captivity. Although none of them had the slightest inkling of it at the time, there was also a distinctly chilling aspect to their new-found paradise, that lay just beneath its idyllic exterior. Not long after the Wehrmacht had marched into Poland in 1939, the machinery for Nazi Germany's systematic programme of extermination of the mentally disabled had been set in motion. Before the war's end, over seventy thousand of those deemed to serve no useful purpose to the Reich had been 'relocated' and summarily euthanised. Given the circumstances, it was only a matter of time before the quiet sanctuary of Liebenau was targeted as a potential source of supply. For decades, the Franciscan nuns in charge of Liebenau had offered a safe haven to hundreds of mentally ill patients of all ages requiring specialised care and attention. It had long since acquired a reputation as an exemplary institution dedicated to serving the needs of its patients in every way possible, but a drastic change was about to take place. The first day of July 1940 saw the sudden and unceremonial removal of 57 selected patients to the Grafeneck death camp. In the coming months over five hundred more hapless souls would follow them to a similar fate.[4]

Then, in October 1940, on the specific orders of SS Reichsführer Heinrich Himmler, the Liebenau facility was officially designated as an internment camp for the civilians of countries who were at war with the German Reich but had not yet been occupied by the Wehrmacht. Henceforth Liebenau would fall under the jurisdiction of officials in the local region of Württemburg. Its new occupants would be women who, for the most part, were citizens of Great Britain and the British

Commonwealth. Someone in the upper echelons of German diplomacy had decided that their presence there would constitute a kind of bargaining chip in the event of the need for a prisoner-of-war exchange. Only in the months ahead would the women interned there begin to discover the horror of what had taken place there prior to their arrival one rainy afternoon.

News of their arrival had preceded them, and a number of the women and children already interned at Liebenau gave the newcomers a rousing welcome, complete with cups of hot tea, bread, butter and jam, in true British fashion. It also turned out to be 'mail day', so there was just time for each of the Zamzamers to write a postcard home – the first communication allowed them since they had been taken prisoner. Then, to top all this excitement, the new arrivals were issued Red Cross parcels. Altogether it had turned out to be an entirely memorable day.

The three Levitts were allotted a small room on the fourth floor of Josefshaus, which they shared with another *Zamzam* passenger, Norah McWhannel, and her two-year-old daughter, Sarah. After everyone had unpacked and settled in, each of the new arrivals was required to answer questions concerning her nationality in order that all could be properly registered by Miss Booth, the designated head of the camp – a woman known officially as the camp captain and the person who dealt with all official correspondence. In this capacity, Miss Booth acted as intermediary between the neutral US embassy, which was charged with protecting British interests, and the German regional official, Herr Inspektor Thomma, who made regular visits to the camp. It was the latter, of course, who had both first and last word on the affairs of the camp and its inhabitants.

When the Liebenau premises were first expropriated in 1940 for use as a place of confinement for women holding British passports, the silver-haired Miss Booth (purportedly the granddaughter of the founder of the Salvation Army), who had been taken prisoner in Warsaw during the German invasion in the early autumn of 1939 – had been singled out to assume the role of go-between for the internees in their dealings with the regional inspector and Gestapo officials. Despite intermittent grumblings from certain quarters about her occasionally authoritarian manner, her intrinsic decency and organisational capabilities stood her in good stead with both the nuns and the internees. And in the end, the quality of Miss Booth's sound leadership undoubtedly helped to make life easier for everyone confined inside the barbed wire that served as a daily reminder that they were, after all, prisoners of war.

Although there were a few Jewish women and children holding British passports who had already been interned at Liebenau, during her debriefing with Miss Booth, Kathleen had no intention of breaking the silence she had maintained since boarding the *Zamzam* in New York Harbour. They were British citizens who had sought refuge from the Blitz with relatives in Montreal and now, due to circumstances completely beyond her control, she and her children had become pawns in a senseless series of misadventures at the hands of their German captors. Fortunately she was able to present her situation in a credibly confident manner and – for the moment – there were no further questions.

Many months later an unsolicited and unwelcome parcel from a Jewish relief agency addressed to Mrs Kathleen Levitt became the source of a frightening brush with the local Gestapo officials, who immediately subjected the recipient to an intimidating interrogation. The Kommandant, in particular, was full of accusations delivered at the top of his voice and embellished with histrionic gestures, but in the end, it was all to no avail. To her everlasting credit, Kathleen had succeeded in putting up an extraordinarily good front and professed – in all truth – that she was totally at a loss to explain how her name could possibly have found its way onto that particular organisation's list of recipients. It was, she resolutely maintained, obviously a case of mistaken identity. How could anyone suspect her of being Jewish when she was the mother of two children with blonde hair and blue eyes? And although his original suspicions were more or less put to rest, the Kommandant decided that a thorough search of their luggage should be undertaken as final proof that Kathleen Levitt had nothing to hide.

As a last desperate measure, he even questioned Norah McWhannel, in the hope of finding some sort of incriminating evidence, but once again he was thwarted. The case was closed. In fact, Kathleen never did discover the identity of the original source of the parcel, but after having come through the Gestapo's gruelling 'third degree' with flying colours, she certainly wasted no time in reaching into her handbag for a cigarette and inhaling deeply. It had been too close for comfort – especially given the fact that only recently one of the Jewish families from Poland had suddenly disappeared from the camp in the middle of the night without a trace, their fate unknown.[5]

The daily round and common task

In all probability, the only thing Liebenau's mixed bag of over three hundred women had in common with one another was a British passport. There were, for instance, several Little Sisters of the Poor, from an English order of charitable nuns who had been picked up from their convents in France. There were cabaret singers, dancers and actresses, apprehended here and there in Holland, Belgium and France. And there were many women from Germany and the occupied countries who had lived their entire lives there, some speaking not a word of English, and holding British passports through the mere accident of birth or marriage. Their common bond was the reality that every last one of these women was the victim of a war about which they knew little and understood less, but each lived in the hope that peace would soon be miraculously restored and they would be free to resume their lives where they had left off.

Not unexpectedly, communal living also produced the occasional unpleasant side effect. When young Peter Levitt became the first in the camp to be the victim of an outbreak of head lice, the memory of it remained fixed in his mind for all time. The question of precisely how or where he had acquired them was never resolved. One possibility was the sandpit located under the large chestnut tree beside Josefshaus, where he spent many happy hours digging and sifting. In any case, within a matter of days more children and adults had become similarly afflicted, and to his chagrin Peter was singled out as a prime suspect. After all, was he not one of the recently arrived *Zamzam* jailbirds who had been confined for weeks in filthy insect-ridden police cells? As the first to be stricken, all fingers naturally pointed towards Peter as cause of the infestation.

As a result, for several weeks afterwards, all those who had been part of the *Zamzam* group became, by default, the unfortunate pariahs of the camp. One after the other, they were each meticulously searched – hair by hair– by the camp's volunteer nurse, for even one tiny nit clinging to a single strand of hair could produce a small army of these nasty parasitic creatures. The prescribed treatment was either a shaved head or a daily washing in a solution of hot water and vinegar, with the latter being selected as the lesser of two evils.[6]

As part of the camp routine, once a week those who wished to join in could go on an organised tramp through the German countryside and the woods under the watchful eye of some of the camp guards. There were also attempts made to organise some kind of educational experience for the fifteen or so children in camp, and at one point they even had a classroom of sorts, but as far as young Peter was concerned it was essentially a waste of time. He could neither read nor write, and was still stuttering on occasion.

When it came to food, although it was probably nourishing enough, the daily fare at Liebenau was something less than appetising, and from what Peter remembers, potatoes and cabbages were the basic ingredients. Had it not been for the bonanza of the internees' bi-monthly Red Cross parcels, they would have been hard pressed to subsist on the bland monotony of the camp diet.

There is no question about the delight with which the *Zamzam* survivors received their first Red Cross parcels. Kitsi Strachan's description of this occasion is a testament to the enormous difference these parcels made to the morale of the prisoners of war who received them:

> It is impossible to describe my emotions on opening this box, as my eyes fell on the receipt card directed to that familiar address – 95 Wellesley Street, Toronto. For almost the first time, a wave of homesickness swept over me for family, friends and for all things Canadian... And it seemed incredibly wonderful that in an hour of real need, I should receive this gift which had come to me so many thousands of miles over the sea. With its arrival, I felt a special message of hope and cheer and the careful planning and packing of its contents spoke of the many people all over Canada who had the interest and the welfare of prisoners of war at heart.[7]

Similar emotions are reflected in Olga Guttormson's ecstatic response to the regular Red Cross bounty arriving at Liebenau from far and wide:

> Food! Food from England, Scotland, Canada, and our American friends. Tinned meats and vegetables, jams, marmalade, tea, coffee, chocolate, raisins, butter and canned milk... In a German prison camp, the Red Cross represents Life itself. It provides food where there is none to be bought. It is bales of cloth for

dresses and coats. Even the twine tied around the parcels could be braided together and made into shoes. The tins could be used for cooking...Every two weeks all of the internees at the Camp received these parcels from afar – Jews, Poles, English, Australians, Dutch, French, Czechs – anyone of any nationality.[8]

After the division of the spoils, Kathleen Levitt proved to be particularly resourceful when it came to the fine art of bartering. Since, between the three of them, they received three Red Cross parcels, they had an excess of cigarettes, so Kathleen would exchange cigarettes through the guards for fresh eggs from the local farmers. These would then be consumed raw by mixing them with Klim – a sweet tinned milk powder which came in the Red Cross parcels from their relations in Canada. There was a constant craving for something sweet, and the chocolate lovers in the camp would usually have their precious bar demolished before the day was out. At one point, Kathleen even managed to get Peter to a local dentist, which she was able to pay for out of her regular monthly stipend of 10 reichsmarks. Each of the *Zamzam* survivors in the camp received the same amount from the Canadian government, courtesy of the American embassy in Berlin, which acted as the conduit to the beneficiaries of this largesse.[9]

Gradually as the freshness of June subsided and the heat of high summer descended, life at Liebenau settled into a routine of sorts. Schooling for the children, Sunday devotional services in English in one of the dormitories, and daily mass for the Roman Catholic internees. In addition, every prisoner was expected to pitch in and make herself useful in one capacity or another. Whether it was scrubbing toilets, polishing floors, peeling enough vegetables to feed six hundred mouths or helping out with the laundry and ironing, there were more than enough tasks to go around.

And, not surprisingly, all this physical activity combined with the fresh country air and a surplus of leisure time made for increased appetites. On each floor there was a small kitchen with a tiny electric stove on which anyone craving something to eat or drink could supplement the camp rations by preparing a little snack for themselves. Kitsi remembers that there was hardly a minute in the day when the little stove was not in use, and that a schedule eventually had to be drawn up for each room's morning and afternoon cup of tea.

> Without much persuasion, one fell easily into the habit of delicious little snacks at almost any hour of the day – a handful of raisins, perhaps, or a nice fat Canadian biscuit topped with cheese. After lunch we mixed up a 'Liebenau Special' – a frothy concoction of powdered milk, cocoa, sugar and water which rivaled the best milk shakes of any soda fountain. 'Not good for the liver, my dears,' warned one of the older members of our party, but we considered it well worth the risk... Any anniversary or birthday served as an excuse for a party and then it was time for the experienced cooks to exercise their ingenuity producing the most wonderful cakes and cookies with at least one important ingredient missing... The artists in our midst produced place cards and arranged the flowers collected on the afternoon walk. Sometimes we could buy beer in the canteen and then toasts would follow the feast.[10]

For her volunteer hours, Isabel opted for half days on kitchen duty and found it quite agreeable to sit on a bench in the summer warmth peeling and preparing vegetables along with the companionable Little Sisters of the Poor, who laughed a lot among themselves. And then there was Schwester Sidonia, with her beloved pet duckling. Even when full-grown, the chances of Donald ever being taken from beneath her protective wing to be served up for someone's supper appeared slim.

Because of her nursing background and experience, it seemed only natural that Olga would volunteer for full-time service in the care of the sick – a service which she performed with the utmost devotion. Then in the evenings, with equal dedication, she studied to perfect her knowledge of the Zulu language in anticipation of the day when she could return to her mission in South Africa.

One of her special patients was a young British mother-to-be who had been taken prisoner at sea just a month or so before the *Zamzam* came under attack. In fact, she had been languishing for several weeks in Bordeaux prior to the captives' arrival there, and accompanied the group of 28 from prison to prison en route to Liebenau. Her husband had been accidentally shot and killed during an uprising in the hold of their prison ship as they sailed up the Garonne towards Bordeaux. Although she repeatedly asked after him, she was told nothing until after the ship's arrival in Bordeaux, when she learned that he had been unceremoniously buried at sea two days earlier. She was then given his coat and taken off to await relocation to an internment camp. As luck would have it, her destination was the peaceful refuge of Liebenau, where – in her hour of need – she came under Olga's kind and compassionate care and gave birth to a baby girl in a nearby hospital in December.

Another of Olga's patients was young Julie, whose story deeply affected this warm-hearted woman with her deep faith. Julie had left England in March 1941 as a British escort for a group of English refugee children being evacuated to Australia. After safely depositing her charges there, Julie re-boarded the ship for the return voyage to England, only to fall prey to a German raider somewhere in the Atlantic. After making the rounds of the north German prison camps, she arrived at Liebenau in April 1941, but was taken ill shortly after her arrival, and was then misdiagnosed. Before the error could be rectified, much to Olga's distress, her patient's case of dysentery had reached the point of no return, and within six months Julie was pronounced dead. News of her death quickly spread through the camp, and with it the realisation that Julie was, in fact, a peripheral victim of the war from which the women of Liebenau felt relatively removed and isolated.

The arrival of mail was by far the most anticipated moment of the day, since, apart from German radio reports, there was virtually no means of keeping in touch with the world at large. From time to time news from 'the Outside' filtered into the camp, but its reliability was almost always open to question. Inevitably, there was also a steady supply of rumours to be processed in the rumour mill, each with its own indisputable ring of credibility. Churchill and Roosevelt had had a meeting somewhere in the Atlantic. Nine million Germans and Russians had been massed along the Russian–German frontier, and heavy losses were reported on both sides. Which of these so-called reports represented the truth and which were merely the product of wishful thinking was anyone's guess, but generally speaking the tidbits of information available to the women interned at Liebenau were few and far between – and far from reliable at the best of times.

One of the newsflashes that travelled through the camp with lightning speed was word that the German authorities had ordered an analysis of each internee's blood. Those with less than 50 per cent British blood would then be released, while those who could proudly claim more would remain prisoners for the duration of the war.

In fact, from time to time, a few people actually did receive permission to leave, including the two Greek nurses C.T. 'Caty' Sallari and Parasaphino 'Marietta' Polou, who had helped to care for Kathleen during her tedious five weeks of confinement aboard the *Dresden*, but these releases certainly bore no relationship to any blood test. The young nurses were returned to their homeland, and sent back despairing accounts to their friends in the camp about the conditions they found in Nazi-occupied Athens, which was making do with only one ambulance to serve the entire city.

Two other *Zamzam* passengers were also permitted an early departure from the confines of Liebenau. Through diplomatic channels in Berlin, temporary American passports were arranged for the wife and 14-year-old daughter of Reverend T.O. Dosumu, the pastor who had initially been confined with the crew of the Zamzam due to his non-white status. He had been released in May with the Americans in Biarritz, but for some unknown reason his wife and daughter had mistakenly been relegated to join the band of 28 women and children who zigzagged their way through Germany for internment in Liebenau. After a relatively brief stay in Berlin, mother and daughter were repatriated to the United States and a joyful homecoming.[11]

Perhaps the only truly reliable source of outside news that escaped Nazi censorship was Benedicte Wilhjelm, whom the Canadians affectionately christened 'the Great Dane'. Miss Wilhjelm was the secretary of the YMCA, based in Berlin, who visited the camp every month or so. Although all the branches of the YMCA and YWCA in Germany had long since been closed, the YMCA was permitted to continue its work by providing assistance to prisoners of war, largely through the singular efforts of the association's remarkable secretary. With the co-operation of her Berlin office, scribbled messages could be delivered by Miss Wilhjelm from husbands in prison camps in north Germany to their wives who were interned in the South and vice versa. Thanks to her efforts on their behalf, two Canadian wives from the Zamzam group – Vida Steele and Allison 'Jamie' Henderson – became grateful participants in this morale-boosting arrangement. At this point, however, no one had any idea that their initial contact with this tireless advocate of those who had had the misfortune of falling into enemy hands would later develop into a warm friendship.

And while the general atmosphere of a convent boarding school for grown women prevailed at Liebenau, Isabel was convinced that the internees inevitably invested the place with something of their composite personality. From her perspective, the resulting mixture of things sacred and secular was occasionally the source of comic relief.

A life-sized crucified Christ hung near the counter of the Camp Canteen, under which the internees bargained with the presiding German sister for what she had been able to buy at the fast depleting village stores: anything from a pair of panties to a dill pickle. Over this counter, too, was dispensed the cigarette allowance which came to the internees from the Red Cross. I've never come across any biblical reference to the smoking habit, but I felt vaguely uncomfortable every time I received my tins of Gold Flakes under the very eyes of that tortured figure. Still, the good German nuns must have seen nothing incongruous, or surely they would have removed Him.[12]

Neither were Isabel's intellect and powers of description limited to the mundane matters of day-to-day existence. This is revealed in her silent musings on the bizarre situation in which they had become involuntary participants.

What good on earth has it done Germany to have Liebenau Women's Internment Camp? Not that its establishment caused much trouble to those responsible. They simply gave orders, one day at the beginning of the War, to the German nuns in charge of Liebenau, which heretofore had been an asylum for German mental and physical deficients – men, women and crippled children. And which henceforth was to house, as well, British interned women and children. To make room for the latter, a certain proportion of the former were removed. Rumour had it – though I have no substantiation – that the removal was more than temporary – that it was the end of their troubles on this earth for those poor lunatics.

The German Sisters may have felt badly about losing some of their former charges. But this arbitrary disposal of things was so much better than what might have happened. They had lived for years in the daily fear of their convent's being closed, like many others, with no future for themselves but the streets or the Führer's factories. So when the first internees turned up at Liebenau's gates, their hands were figuratively kissed by the German nuns; here was a gift from God, a sign that the Order's precarious existence could continue, even if still precariously.

By the time we reached Liebenau, some eighteen months later, emotionalism had passed, routine had set in, and the

German Sisters were impersonal wardresses, showing no partisan favouritism – unless a shade more warmth to their mental charges than to us. It was wiser so – with the collective eye of the Guard-house always upon them. A sort of armed neutrality existed between the nuns and the Wache, who were the half-dozen uniformed Gestapo guards in charge of the Camp, and who, in turn, were responsible to the Herr Inspektor, a member of the high-sounding Württemberg Ministry of the Interior.

I had always the feeling that the nuns need not have stood in any great awe of the Wache, who must have been a semi-moronic lot anyway, to have rated this pansy job of looking after a Women's Camp.[13]

A sudden turnaround

For all his bluster and self-importance, Isabel was quick to spot the tactics employed by the nuns in order to be assured of the Herr Inspektor's goodwill and his smiles of approval. Handled with care, there was always the possibility that he could be charmed into submission:

> Though the Herr Inspektor was a small man in what he thought were big boots, he was vulnerable too. The Sisters need only give him their best convent lunch, on his fortnightly inspection day, and his favour was won – at least as far as they were concerned. Eating was important in Germany that year – and good eating, very difficult to find.[14]

The Herr Inspektor spoke no English – although there were those who thought this may have been a ruse on his part – but, in any event, every interview was conducted in German and an interpreter was on hand in the event that the person presenting a plea spoke no German. To those in the camp who were obliged to have dealings with him, the Herr Inspektor was known to be a creature of unpredictable temper and sadistic instincts. In order to avoid seeing him in person, the camp captain, Miss Booth, made a point of communicating with him in writing, with the exception of occasions when it was strictly necessary. And, as Isabel noted, the camp interpreters also handled him with kid gloves.

> On the days of his visits, a line-up of women could be seen waiting outside his office. There was Mrs X who asked to be allowed to return to her villa in the South of France with her delicate, crippled, highly strung daughter... There was Madame Z, a half-French, half-Italian opera singer, whose British passport was only the mistake of having acquired a British husband – long since divorced. She must return to Italy as her bel canto voice was suffering... There were three Red Cross Sisters caught after the fall of France, who had been told since the beginning that they would be released any day.[15]

As the late spring turned into summer, Isabel subtly began to apply her own appreciable powers of persuasion in her dealings with Herr Inspektor Thomma. The women of the *Zamzam* were the fifth and last group of sea victims to have arrived at the camp. And – among the Canadians in particular – there was growing concern that their attempts to communicate in writing with the appropriate authorities in Canada were not getting past the German censors assigned to undertake the perusal and culling of any and all mail that left the camp premises. If access to the American consul in Berlin could somehow be arranged, surely the predicament of the poor, helpless Canadian women in Liebenau would receive the attention it deserved? It was obvious that the longer they remained sequestered in the hinterland, the less possibility there would be of any sort of intervention by the Canadian government on behalf of a handful of women trapped inside Nazi Germany.

The well-founded suspicion that their chances of any steps being taken to secure their release were diminishing by the day helped to galvanise the Canadians' determination to persuade Herr Inspector Thomma that it was imperative that they be sent on to Berlin. With Isabel in the forefront, increasingly these tactful but persistent queries and pleas became a source of almost impossible aggravation for the beleaguered Inspektor. The question was – how long could he hold out in the face of this ceaseless campaign, and when would he arrange for them to be put on the next train to Berlin. Certainly, nothing would please him more than to rid the camp of this band of tiresome and determined women, but did he dare to take matters into his own hands?

By mid-September, the Canadian *Zamzam* survivors had already endured close to five long months of imprisonment at the hands of their German captors, yet they had steadfastly refused to abandon the faint hope of being released. Behind the scenes, the wheels of inter-governmental communiqués had, in fact, been slowly grinding towards a solution to end their enforced confinement. They were – after all – hapless civilians caught up in unforeseen events that had conspired against them almost since the day they sailed out of New York Harbour.

Then came an indication from those in positions of higher authority in Berlin that perhaps there was a real possibility of an early solution. This was based – at least in part – on confidential information that certain German women who had been marooned in Canada since 1939 had not yet been selected for internment. This being the case, why should Canadian women trapped in the Third Reich not be accorded similar latitude? The Inspektor had been handed a way out of his dilemma.[16] The Canadians could be released. There was, however, no mention of any specific date.

In her final interview with Thomma, Isabel was armed with the current scuttlebutt doing the rounds at the time, that there was talk of the possibility of the release of the Canadians at Liebenau, so she decided to seize the bull by the horns and ask him outright if there was any truth to this rumour.

He answered my question mildly by asking one in return. 'Are you a Canadian?' He asked this as if a Canadian were some sort of rare bird – not quite nice to know. He digested me mentally, then asked for my passport. Finally came the staggering announcement that there truly was a chance of repatriation and that we should bring all our passports to him and an application for release, giving some financial guarantee.[17]

Having made his decision, the Inspektor was not about to waste any time setting the wheels of the Canadians' exodus from Liebenau into motion.

Within less than twenty-four hours, he had inscribed each of our passports with a page of German text that was a diabolic inspiration on his part and totally misleading to us.

He wrote: 'The holder of this passport, by notice of the Württemberg Ministry of the Interior in Stuttgart, is today released as a Canadian citizen from the Civilian Internment Camp Liebenau, district of Friedrichshafen, to proceed to Berlin; there to have the American Embassy, as the protecting power of her country, arrange everything further regarding the return trip to Canada; also to have the trip to Canada financed by this Embassy.'

This was followed by a short paragraph obliging me to register with the Foreign Police in Berlin – dated Sept. 13, 1941 – and the document is signed and attested with the name of the Herr Inspektor and the stamp of the German Eagle. It was clever, I'm bound to admit – for it allows its perpetrator the loophole of this interpretation: '...to have the American Embassy... arrange everything further (if they can!)...' But it baffled the American Embassy, and embarrassed the German Foreign Office – since no one seemed to know whence came the authority for this cleverness.[18]

On the afternoon of 13 September, after a frenzied attempt to pack what was needed and leave behind items of possible use to the good friends they would soon be parted from, the members of a select group of 14 women were ready to begin their hopeful journey to Berlin. In addition to the original seven Canadians taken from the *Zamzam* – Kitsi

Strachan, Isabel Guernsey, Clara Guilding, Olga Guttormson, Allison Henderson, Vida Steele and Doreen Turner – two other Canadian women, Catherine Scherfe and Gwendolyne Foreshaw – who had both been trapped in Germany when war broke out, were included among the prisoners scheduled for release. Five South African women rounded out their number. Two were former *Zamzam* passengers – Violet Hankins from Toronto, who had married a South African doctor, and Helen Hyatt, a teacher from Cape Town. The identity of the other three remains undocumented. Because their government had already interned a number of German women, those holding Australian passports were automatically slated for further detention in Liebenau in the event of a prisoner-of-war exchange.

Just a few days before this sudden change in the status quo at Liebenau, a Red Cross shipment had arrived, and it became an immediate priority to ensure that those who lacked coats and dresses were properly equipped before heading into the heart of the Third Reich. Word of meagre food rations also prompted them to take along as many extra supplies as they could possibly carry.

Peter Levitt retains a faint memory of the entire camp turning out at the Liebenau gates to see off the chosen 14 as they clambered into a high van – rather like a covered wagon – and rolled away towards the railway station, leaving a sea of faces and waving hands in their wake.

At the time, he had no inkling that he and his sister could also have been part of the Berlin brigade, but he is certain that his mother's decision that they should remain together in Liebenau was undoubtedly the most sensible course of action. Envisaging the prospect of caring for two small children in the midst of war-torn Berlin, Kathleen had no qualms whatever about the wisdom of her decision. It might mean a longer wait until their release, but the well-being of the children was her ultimate priority.

After many false starts, in October 1942, the three Levitts eventually became part of a Red Cross exchange initiative that involved some German Templer prisoners who were being held in Palestine. (The Templers were a small religious sect founded in South Germany in the nineteenth century, and certain of its members had become known as Nazi sympathisers.) The Levitts' extended journey to freedom took them through Vienna, Turkey, Palestine, Cairo and finally to South Africa, where Kathleen's husband, Lionel, was stationed with the Royal Air Force. In retrospect, she always maintained that she had never regretted spending those extra months with the children in the peace and tranquillity of Liebenau. It had been the right choice.

5

Stranded in Berlin

14 September 1941–12 June 1942

Hotel Wartburg

As the train clattered northward towards Berlin, the now-seasoned *Zamzam* travellers were in a state of high anticipation about their impending release. If they had known of the incredibly long and drawn-out series of complex bureaucratic negotiations that lay ahead, their mood might well have been slightly less optimistic. Crowded together in a tiny railway compartment and corridor, after a seemingly endless overnight journey, they finally reached their destination – Berlin's Anhalter railway station – the morning after their departure from Liebenau.

Filled with the fresh exhilaration of new-found freedom, they were totally unprepared for the shock that awaited them. No one was there to greet them! Surrounded by their luggage, the exhausted and bewildered little clutch of foreigners stood rooted to the spot as they watched the throngs of passengers streaming off purposefully in all directions. They had been given assurances that they would be met at the station, but it soon became obvious that the wire announcing their arrival had either gone astray or never been sent. What to do? Where to go? Perhaps a telephone call to the American embassy was in order? Isabel seized the initiative.

> It was a strange feeling to find ourselves alone, on our own, unguarded, for the first time in Reich territory – nobody seeing nor caring about this invasion of the Enemy Capital by fourteen women. We were unarmed, of course, except for our Red Cross food parcels.
>
> I was tired after standing most of sixteen hours on a crowded train and I have never liked strange telephone booths. In particular I didn't much fancy facing one at eight o'clock on a grey Sunday morning in a huge unknown station. But it had to be done. Luckily a German telephone-book was much like any other – and thank heaven it was a dial telephone, so that the German language had not to be wrestled with as well. And more thanks to heaven for the American voice at the other end, which said 'No, there had been no word of our coming at the Embassy, but it would inform the proper person that fourteen women awaited his attention at the Anhalter station.'
>
> Considerably relieved, I came out of the booth to find two of my companions already engaged in conversation with a strange woman, who turned out to be an American journalist, and our first benefactor in Berlin. She had heard English being spoken, had decided with quick journalistic perception that we were something new on the Berlin horizon, and had stopped to inquire. She was catching a train, so we saw her off while she advised us to call the American Church if the Embassy didn't turn up and pressed some perforated strips of paper into our hands with the parting words: 'Here, you'll need these. Sorry I can't do more.' The perforated strips were bread tickets – our introduction to food cards in Berlin.[1]

Ravenously hungry after their long journey, while waiting for their contact from the American embassy to turn up, the 14 women descended en masse on the station restaurant and put their newly acquired coupons to immediate use. Their first taste of real freedom after five months of imprisonment. It was almost too good to be true!

Before long, Wary Perry, the third secretary at the American embassy arrived in his smart little cabriolet to welcome the new arrivals, and took Isabel off with him in search of accommodation for 14 unexpected newcomers. The prospects of a quick solution were far from promising, but by a stroke of good luck they were able to locate two hotels on Anhalterstrasse in the vicinity of the station, and the process of getting everyone settled quickly got underway. Eight of the women were directed to one location, six to the other. Isabel describes the experience:

And so we were initiated into hotel life in Berlin. It was quite an experience, moving into 'The Wart' (our abbreviation for The Wartburg Hotel). As well, it was reassuring to be escorted by the American Third Secretary, instead of by a Nazi policeman, and asked to register, in quite a normal fashion, at the hotel desk. The last time we had registered had been as guests of Herr Baum in Wesermunde Jail. Dear Wary Perry – like all young career diplomats, he had the fat living bonus allowed to those on foreign service and 'The Wart' no doubt looked pretty sordid to him.

But I shall always be grateful to him for his choice of hotels. Of the six of us who moved into 'The Wart', four lived there eight months. It was old, dark and not very clean; it was under-staffed and ill-equipped – our sheets were changed perhaps every six weeks; and it cost much more than we could afford. Nevertheless its proprietors were decent to us and long-suffering at a time when hotel-keepers could afford to be tough, for rooms all over Berlin were at a premium. They loaned us hotel cutlery and dishes and allowed electric cookers in our rooms – until we blew out the fuses with such regularity that we wore out the patience of the day and night clerks who had to fix them – and the electric light bill tripled itself in two months. Then they called a halt on stoves in rooms and said we must use the three-burner gas range in the hotel kitchen. That was really better for us anyway; for our health, and for the general atmosphere of our rooms during the cold winter months when we could bear our windows open only if in bed protected by our eiderdowns. But the trek up and down the four flights from our attic aerie sometimes counter-acted the desired effect of food.

We were six when we moved into 'The Wart', and three rooms were assigned to us. There was no planned choice in the matter – it just happened that Jamie and Doreen [Allison Henderson of Winnipeg and Doreen Turner of Toronto] registered first, and so they were given Room 7, which was on the first floor up. It was quite a grand bedroom, or so it seemed to us, after our crowded quarters in prison trains, jails and Liebenau's dormitories. It had brass bedsteads with a purple pomp of drapery at head and foot to keep the draught out. There were two capacious white-veined black marble basins, with a great expanse of mirror atop. There was a huge wardrobe of some dark wood. And there were bedside tables, with a lamp on one and a telephone on the other. All this following so closely upon Josefshaus, Room 7, was luxury indeed.

We others congratulated Doreen and Jamie on their good luck and proceeded upwards. Two flights more and Vida and Olga found themselves established in Room 28, Kitsi and I in Room 23. These did not boast the elegance of Room 7. In 'The Wart', as you went up in the air, you went down in the social scale. That was understandable later, when we discovered that regular hotel guests were not encouraged to use the creaking glass-walled elevator – it was the special prerogative of new arrivals, the hotel staff bringing up trays or taking down laundry, or occasional visitors of high estate such as the Wehrmacht.

However, the four of us settled into our more modest nests, satisfied enough. And it was all quite a good arrangement. Room 7, the most impressive, was also the most accessible and so the best in which to receive general callers. Room 28 had the most convenient spacing for setting up a table for six, at which we mostly had our evening meal for the first month, and Vida being the most housewifely and best cook, this was a good thing. That left Room 23 more private, airy and uncrumbed for Kitsi and me. We were the most selfish and most useless – so that was a good thing too.

Of course, we didn't discover all this until later. It was merely happenstance – and we settled in that first day, simply happy to be left to our own resources – six Canadians, free on the top floor of a Berlin hotel – many rungs up the ladder towards civilisation and Home.[2]

Later that evening, the Canadians had their first visitor… the wonderful Miss Wilhjelm of the YWCA who had visited them in Liebenau. What a delight to have this most remarkable middle-aged Danish dynamo in their midst and be able to share with her the joyful celebration of their unexpected release from internment! During the months ahead, Benedicte Wilhjelm would become a lifeline of good faith, as the Canadians' initial hopes of early repatriation were dashed time and again.

At this stage, there was every expectation that it would only be a matter of a few weeks before the official word would come through via the US embassy and they would be homeward bound. But since their visit to Berlin would be relatively brief, they might as well enjoy this opportunity for leisurely sightseeing as much as possible. Perhaps it was more than a little providential that they had no inkling whatsoever of just how long they would have to remain there and how well they would come to know the many facets of life among the Berliners.

The following morning, Isabel received a message from Miss Wilhjelm that she should be ready within an hour to accompany her to the American embassy.[3] From the outset, their friend and mentor had singled out Isabel as her liaison with the Canadian contingent, and Isabel was full of hope that this – her first visit to the embassy of the United States – would be both helpful and productive.

After being given a warm welcome at the embassy, Isabel learned that arrangements were being put in place with government officials in Canada for her and her compatriots to receive a monthly draw of 150 reichsmarks each month. The appearance of Scherman and Murphy's article in *Life* magazine had already been widely discussed among the Americans, and when it became known that Isabel was an eye-witness survivor, this vibrant and intelligent addition to the Berlin scene was transformed into the object of much favourable attention.

To begin with, the majority of the American population in Berlin had been narrowed down to men who were either single or whose wives had already returned home. The prospect of meeting newcomers – and moreover female newcomers – who bore the potential to brighten their days – and possibly their nights – resulted in an immediate invitation to all the survivors of the *Zamzam* to attend a cocktail party later that same afternoon.

At their first Berlin party, replete with military and naval personnel and set against the elegant background of the former French Club in Budapesterstrasse, the 14 oddly assorted women of the *Zamzam* decked out in their rescued shipwreck clothing became the object of great interest and admiration. Only a week earlier, the thought of being able to socialise in the civilised world again after so many months in captivity was something totally unimaginable. Yet here they were – the very centre of attention, with the promise of more good times to come.

At one point during the course of the evening, Isabel was interviewed by CBS correspondent Harry Flannery, who later reported on the air that he had talked in Berlin with a blue-eyed, smartly dressed young woman in her thirties who was a survivor of the *Zamzam*.[4] Friends in the United States. who heard the broadcast were heartened by the news that Isabel had come through with her habitual panache and were able to put to rest any concerns they might have had that the experience had transformed her into a wan and haggard shadow of her former self.

By the time the interview was over, the party had almost broken up, and Isabel was invited out to be royally wined and dined in the company of an assortment of high-ranking American officers – the playboys of the Berlin embassy. Later she would turn down an invitation to stay the night – possibly an invitation made with only the best of intentions, but she chose the high road and returned to her roost in 'The Wart' to join Kitsi and the others bearing a gift of delicious pears from 'the boys' at the supper club to 'the girls' of 'The Wart'. She was also well aware of the disapproval her overnight absence might have precipitated. The common travails they shared had slowly but surely created an incongruous bond of mutual respect and loyalty among these enormously disparate women of the *Zamzam* and, for Isabel, at that stage, any possibility of disturbing this valued and delicate balance would have gone very much against the grain.

And although the new arrivals were generally pleased by the friendly reception they had been given by the Americans during their second day in Berlin, they were left in some doubt about further concrete developments from that quarter concerning the timing and details related to their expected repatriation. They would simply have to remain hopeful that their patience would soon be rewarded. Isabel, for one, had the distinct impression that the embassy staff had not actually concerned themselves to any great extent about the plight of the Canadians. At that point, it seemed obvious to her that they were preoccupied with concerns about what the future had in store for the diminishing number of Americans left holding the fort in Berlin.[5]

Settling into the *Damenstift*

In the days and weeks to come, their contact with Miss Wilhjelm provided the Canadians of the Hotel Wartburg with the kind of practical assistance that saved them from many potential pitfalls as they gradually settled into the rhythm and routine of life in the German capital. The fact that – at this point – none of them spoke more than monosyllabic German also put them at a distinct disadvantage in dealing with the everyday realities of their new life. Isabel is full of praise for their adoptive 'Great Dane':

It was she who taught me, on that very first morning trip to the American Embassy, that by walking one long block from our hotel I could save 10 pfennigs on the street-car fare – Berlin street-car lines being zoned. And she told us which were the best of the cheaper restaurants – even one where we could get bread with our meals at no extra charge. Such minor economies were necessary on our relief allowance.

She got us our first food cards and instructed us how and where best to use them and how to get them for ourselves the next time. She even collected our special green egg-cards several times and managed to get us an egg apiece fortnightly for a while.

She took us in a body to register with the local police where we were given long and complicated forms to fill out. And when she suggested that we take them away with us, to be completed and returned later that day, the policeman in charge complied very readily. Then after she asked if each of us must return her paper individually, the policeman shouted: 'No! For God's sake! ... Keep those women away from here!'[6]

Once the various ration tickets had been acquired, Olga and Vera went off together on an exploratory foray to discover if they would actually be able to purchase something in the shops and bring it home with them. Since all food and clothing in Germany had been rationed since a week after the outbreak of war, almost nothing could be purchased without presenting the required number of small squares of perforated paper or a printed ration card. And even at this relatively early stage in the war, food shortages in Germany had become severe enough that the civilian population had virtually been cut back to half-rations.[7] Without the necessary cards or coupons it was impossible to purchase any meat, butter, margarine, milk, vegetables, sugar, flour, bread, biscuits, coffee, pudding powders, macaroni, rice or fruit: in other words, practically anything and everything remotely edible. However, as Olga notes,

Even with our ration cards, we could not always obtain food. Fruit was only available on certain days and we often went from one store to another only to be notified that they were all sold out... Many German housewives entering a food market hastily scanned the store and then fell in at the end of the longest line without even knowing what they were lining up for. But a line always meant that, for a limited time, some sort of food was available... The week before Christmas we waited in line for two hours to get a small package of raisins.[8]

As the Zamzamers had already discovered during the course of their freedom breakfast at the Anhalter Bahnhof shortly after their arrival in Berlin, even in restaurants many foods could not be served unless ration tickets were first presented to the waiter to be exchanged in the kitchen for the specified quantities of food requested. Nor was Olga very impressed by the quality of the food at the best of times.

The bread was mealy and hard and there was no real milk except for small children. The rest of Berlin used a thin milk substitute. Coffee and tea were almost impossible to obtain and were replaced by a variety of cheaper substitutes. A spice substitute was used to replace the exhausted supply of pepper. Fats of all kind and butter were also in scarce supply, since fats were used for munitions... Groceries could often not be purchased unless the customer supplied his or her own paper bags and these were in very short supply. Absolutely no gasoline nor rubber could be procured with the result that there were no cars on the Berlin streets with the exception of those driven by Nazi officials, doctors and foreign diplomats.

Smokers, as well, were driven to desperation by the everlasting shortage of tobacco and cigarettes... Cigar stores were only open during certain hours of each day and it was not unusual to see a hundred people standing in line out on the street waiting to purchase a package of cigarettes... Store windows were often full, but inside there was nothing. Requests for cups and saucers, clocks, watches, fountain pens, paper, cameras and film were all met with the same reply, 'Wehrmacht'. Everything went to the army while Germany's civilian population merely worked and waited.[9]

As for clothing, after three years of strict rationing the shortages were becoming acute. All old coats and shoes had to be turned in before new ones could be purchased. No leather goods were for sale anywhere within the Third Reich. Although for a brief period after the fall of France, silk stockings and new supplies of cosmetics came onto the market, most women and girls were now forced to return to the standard glamourless heavy cotton stockings. Nor were lipstick or rouge anywhere to be found. It made for a drab and discouraging outlook.[10]

But despite the tiresome necessity of trudging from one shop to the next, the Canadians never ceased to be amazed by the surprisingly cordial treatment they received while making their daily rounds. Isabel remarks on this at some length.

> It was an interesting and surprising feature of our life there: that we should have been among the privileged of some of Berlin's small shop-keepers. For vegetables, we generally frequented the establishment operated by Herr Kiss, because he sometimes favoured us. His shop was most unprepossessing – a dark little hole-in-the-wall, with nothing on view but potatoes and a few tired-looking bunches of mixed soup greens. But we soon caught on. You would ask very quietly: 'Gibt es Zwiebeln?' ('Are there any onions?') The idea was to keep it a secret between you and Herr Kiss. In little shops such as his there would be at best a very limited supply of this luxury vegetable, and only if he liked you would he give you any. Naturally he didn't want to advertise this preferential treatment to the world at large, but if there were onions to be had, they were generally ours.
>
> Needless to say, our presence was soon known in the small world in which we shopped. The typical Berliner is frankly curious and without inhibitions about asking questions. Almost without exception, people would smile at us and say: 'We didn't want this War.' And we, who were not only foreigners but the Enemy, would receive milk without cards. I even had a shopkeeper friend who sometimes slipped me white bread on brown bread tickets, and once my whole monthly allowance – all of 125 grams, a quarter pound – of Limburger cheese instead of half-Limburger, half-farmer's cheese which didn't keep for long.[11]

Years later, after she had safely returned to the two children she had left behind in Alberta, Vida also recalled the courtesies extended to the Canadians by the local butcher. As a British POW during World War I, he had retained only good memories of his treatment while in their hands and was delighted to be able to return the favour as best he could.

> But it was almost embarrassing. We would enter the store with many people lined up ahead of us and he would say in English 'Good morning, ladies. Come on up to the front and put your tickets and money in your bag.' A short time later, he would return with our order … This good man would often give us supplies that he denied to others.[12]

Each night at nine o'clock a heavy silence settled over the blacked-out city and, more specifically, over the *Damenstift*. The first film Isabel had seen in Berlin was called *Aufruhr im Damenstift* (Uproar in the Ladies' Home), and this became Isabel's inspiration for the name of their quarters in the Hotel Wartburg. To the Canadians in the *Damenstift*, the nightly blackout was nothing particularly unusual, as they had already experienced blackout conditions at sea when they were crossing the Atlantic on board the *Zamzam* and later during their five weeks of misery as prisoners on the *Dresden*. In Berlin, like moving specks in the oppressive blackness, the city's inhabitants jostled one another in the darkened streets, their passing undertones merging into a low even murmur as people milled in and out of the theatres which continued to operate as if peacetime conditions still prevailed.

For the most part, the films were German, as well as the occasional Italian production and, inevitably, short propaganda films were always included. Newsreel footage of front-line activities seemed to leave the audience sitting in dull apathy with no signs of emotion. All travel documentaries featured South American countries. From time to time, the film projection would be stopped to allow for the blaring voice of a Nazi official or news commentator to be broadcast over a loudspeaker – a feature that was also a requirement for every department store, concert hall or other public gathering place.

The original jacket of Isabel Guernsey's 1943 account of her wartime misadventure.

Levitt Family archives.

The original Bibby liner SS *Leicestershire*, launched in Belfast in 1909, served as a troopship during World War I and later transported passengers to India before changing hands in 1933 to become the Egyptian-owned SS *Zamzam*.

Copyright John H. Marsh Maritime Collection, Iziko Maritime Centre, Cape Town, South Africa. Photo courtesy of the private collection of Wallace Nolin.

A group of kindred spirits gathers in Recife, Pernambuco, Brazil. Peter and Wendy Levitt are in the foreground, posing with Harry Cawthorne, Ned Laughinghouse, Kathleen Levitt, Charles Murphy, Isabel Guernsey, Paul Burton, Tom Miller and an unidentified passenger.

Levitt family archives.

Kathleen 'Kitsy' Strachan, photographed with her husband Robin on their pre-war honeymoon voyage.

Courtesy of Irma Coucill, Toronto.

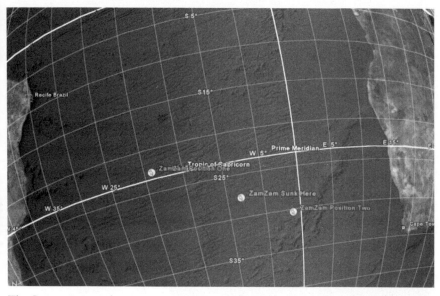

The *Zamzam*'s route from Recife across the South Atlantic towards Cape Town.

Missionaries Ellsworth and Vida Steele with an unidentified companion on board the *Zamzam*.

Steele family archives.

The dreaded German surface raider *Atlantis*, disguised as the Norwegian merchant ship *Tamesis*, which attacked and sank the *Zamzam* on 17 April 1941.

Photo by David E. Scherman, *Life* magazine.

Captain Bernhard Rogge of the Hilfskreuzer *Atlantis* in full dress uniform and wearing his Iron Cross.

Photo by Dr Ulrich Mohr.

The officers of the *Atlantis*, also known by the code name *Ship 16*.

Bundesarchiv-Militärarchiv Freiburg.

Zamzam passengers and crew taking to the lifeboats.

Photo by David E. Schermann, *Life* magazine.

Survivors coming alongside the *Atlantis*.

Photo by Dr Ulrich Mohr.

American missionary Lillian Danielson, posing with her six children before embarking on their voyage to join her husband in Africa aboard the *Zamzam*.

Photo courtesy of Eleanor Anderson (Danielson).

Zamzam passengers view their listing ship from the deck of the *Atlantis* just prior to the detonation of the explosive charges that will send her to the bottom.

Photo by Dr Ulrich Mohr.

Male prisoners in the makeshift quarters in the hold of the German prison ship *Dresden*, where they spent five arduous weeks.

Photo by Dr Ulrich Mohr.

Walter Jaeger, captain of the *Dresden*.

Photo by Dr Ulrich Mohr.

Zamzam survivors arrive in St Jean-de-Luz in German-occupied France.

Photo by David E. Scherman, *Life* magazine.

Internees at Liebenau detention camp displaying their treasured Red Cross packages.

Isabel Guernsey collection.

Peter and Wendy Levitt
enjoying the summer sunshine
at Liebenau.

Levitt family archives.

Newly arrived internees
at Liebenau in June
1941.

Olga Guttormson archives.

Isabel Guernsey
(wearing striped
frock), shown with her
companions peeling
vegetables while on
Liebenau kitchen duty.

Isabel Guernsey collection.

The schoolchildren of Liebenau, including disenchanted student Peter Levitt (second row, left).

Levitt family archives.

Kathleen Levitt (second from the left) enjoying a cigarette and a game of bridge with friends at Liebenau.

Levitt family archives.

Herr Inspektor Thomma, the designated Nazi official in charge of the British detainees held at Liebenau.

Levitt family archives.

A German soldier taking a cigarette break in the doorway of the Liebenau guardhouse.

Levitt family archives.

The document of permission for Kathleen, Peter and Wendy Levitt to leave Germany in October 1942.

Levitt family archives.

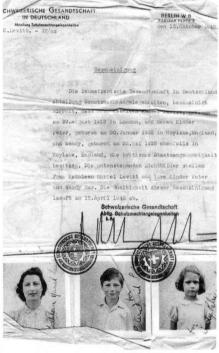

Three of the Canadian residents of the Hotel Wartburg on Anhalterstrasse, Berlin.

Isabel Guernsey collection.

The seven intrepid Canadians posing for a snapshot in Berlin during the winter of 1941–42 (left to right): Kitsi Strachan, Vida Steele, Clara Guilding, Isabel Guernsey, Olga Guttormson, Doreen Turner and Allison 'Jamie' Henderson.

Isabel Guernsey collection.

The crew members of the raider *Atlantis* aboard and alongside a German U-boat after their ship had been sunk in November 1941 by the British battlecruiser HMS *Devonshire*.

Photo by Dr Ulrich Mohr.

The exterior of Berlin's famed Adlon Hotel.

Courtesy of Ullstein Bild.

The bar of the Adlon Hotel, where Isabel Guernsey and Kitsi Strachan met British author P.G. Wodehouse for a pre-Christmas cocktail in December 1941.

Courtesy of Ullstein Bild.

Ethel and P.G. Wodehouse, known to his friends as 'Plum' and to his readers as the creator of Bertie Wooster and Jeeves.

Courtesy of Frances Donaldson.

Rear Admiral Erich Räder, World War I friend and protector of Captain Bernhard Rogge against persecution by Gestapo zealots.

Bundesarchiv-Militärarchiv Freiburg.

Admiral Räder officially honouring the crew members of the *Atlantis* in Berlin after their 655 days at sea.

Photo by Dr Ulrich Mohr.

bassy.

...were assured by the above official that this state-
...cleared us with German authority, the only
...business being to procure the visas necessary for
...return trip. But, on arrival in Berlin, we find
...further official permission than the above-mentioned
...tion in our passports is required before we can
...the country.

      For this we hereby apply.
         Signed, on behalf of the party,
                  Isabel M. Guernsey

...ican Embassy.

A letter signed by Isabel Guernsey on behalf of herself and her fellow Canadians stranded in Berlin.

Official stamp of the German SS Reichsführer and Chief of Police, granting permission for the Canadians to leave Berlin.

: K r ö n 1 n g

Isabel Guernsey and Kitsi Strachan during their brief but idyllic stay in the garden house outside Berlin.

Isabel Guernsey collection.

Peter and Wendy Levitt in Liebenau internment camp, Winter 1942.

Levitt family archives.

Accustomed to the nights of blackness, the days of work and the endless hours of waiting in queues, the Berliners went about the business of living from hand to mouth with singular stoicism. Even the wail of the air-raid sirens did little to shake them from the oppressive gloom of passivity.

Just one week into the newly freed Canadians' stay at 'The Wart', in the early hours of the morning of 20 September, the warning sirens sounded. They were about to experience their first Allied raid. The thought of British and Canadian pilots above, poised to open their bomb bays and drop their payload on the heads of their own people was a bizarre sensation, but no one wasted any time giving it much thought as they sprang into action. It was a clear starlit night, and reports had come through of raids over Bremen and Hamburg. They had all also seen the bombed-out shell of the opera house during their walk with Miss Wilhjelm to the police station when they went for their official registration, so they were well aware it was only a matter of time before Berlin would be the target once again.

> We dressed and hurried to the basement of the hotel. There were a few people already in the specially constructed air-raid shelter. An hour passed and some of the occupants began to grow restless. Many of them ventured back into the courtyard. At 4.00 a.m. we could hear the firing of the anti-aircraft guns which were set up only three blocks from the hotel. At 4.20 the all-clear signal was given and Berlin went back to sleep.[13]

But with each passing day, fears for the future were increasing. As Olga perceptively observed, the German people had given their food, their clothing, their labour, and increasingly they were losing their husbands and their sons, since every man of military age was called to serve. Horror stories from the eastern front were making the rounds of Berlin, including one about a young German soldier who had returned to the city on leave, and chose to take his own life rather than face the grim prospect of being sent back to join his regiment. Whispered rumours of typhus, misery and spreading discontent among the troops were on many people's lips, but the talk was more like sublimated murmurs. People may have thronged the streets but – for the most part – their thoughts remained unspoken. Listeners were everywhere. Gestapo agents, secret service men in plain clothes and informers. They listened in the theatres, by grocery counters, on the streets, in restaurants. Almost no place was safe from these listening ears. Berliners had learned from experience that it was only safe to speak in hushed tones or not at all.

There was little talk in Berlin. People were working and waiting – waiting to secure enough food so they could work the next day. Everywhere – on the streets, in the stores, in the overcrowded hotels and pensions – were the forced labourers brought in from the Nazi-occupied countries to work in the factories. Foreigners, small babies and wounded soldiers were filling the streets of Berlin…After three years of war, the wounded had begun to appear in droves. Young men who had returned from The Front – crippled, blind, with disfigured faces and bodies. They were everywhere. And there were thousands more who did not roam – who had not come back, who would never return from The Front…Instead, the official notices of the fallen began to filter back with increasing regularity.

During the daylight hours, we saw few children over five years of age on the streets. Most were attending Hitler Youth schools and those that we did see were in uniform. They wore them everywhere – at school, at home, at play – for the true hold of the Nazi movement was on the youth of Germany. They were its staunchest supporters…We learned of one German who had been called before the Gestapo for having carelessly criticised the Nazi regime in the confines of his home. He had been reported by his ten-year-old son. To the youth of Germany there was only one loyalty – loyalty to Hitler. This loyalty transcended all ties with home and church. No loyal member of the Nazi party acknowledged any power greater than Hitler. He was the personification of power in Germany and he sought world domination.[14]

In addition to the perpetual string of political rumours, there were also more than enough rumours doing the rounds in the world of housewives and homemakers. As autumn advanced and the nights grew longer, a weekend rumour began circulating that electrical fixtures were in very short supply and would soon be non-existent. This came as especially alarming news to the inhabitants of the *Damenstift*, whose ability to prepare a meal was largely dependent on the hotel's single-coil electrical hot plates that burned out with distressing regularity. By Monday evening, Berlin's supply had been totally decimated, but by Thursday, two of the existing stoves in 'The Wart' had been repaired. It was all a matter of chance. Uncertainty became an integral part of their daily lives.

Every once in a while a particularly amusing rumour would surface, such as the one about the feminine hygiene product Camelia. Word on the street had it that all sales would be discontinued until after the war as it had been requisitioned by the military.

On one occasion, Vida and Olga – with ration cards and coupons in hand – were out in search of the daily provisions for the *Damenstift* when they found themselves the unwilling observers of a highly unsettling scene in a nearby grocery store. A local housewife had made the mistake of raising her voice in protest. As the mother of several children with a working husband – like everyone else – she was accustomed to waiting in line for hours to procure their meagre rations. But this time, when she arrived at the counter and the reply was the same for each item on her list – 'All sold out!' – in her frustration she began to berate the shopkeeper. To Vida and Olga's horror, as if on cue, a Gestapo agent silently stepped out of the line, tapped the woman on the shoulder and ushered her out of the shop. She would learn the hard way that her unpatriotic outburst was not in the best interests of maintaining the morale of the German people. Such breaches of the code of acceptable behaviour must be dealt with instantly as a lesson for all to see.[15]

On the other hand, those first few weeks in Berlin were mainly filled with more agreeable experiences as the *Zamzam* 14 explored the city's many attractions and began making new acquaintances. The news of their presence prompted a number of invitations from within the American community and, in addition to Miss Wilhjelm, the flock acquired another new advocate – the young pastor of the American church. Because of the ongoing withdrawal of Americans from Berlin his parochial duties were now negligible and 'Uncle Stewart' had joined the embassy staff just in time to become the official godfather to the new arrivals from Liebenau. There is no question that this 'admirable young man' made a highly favourable impression on Isabel, who was full of praise for the obvious pleasure he took in ensuring that his newly acquired charges were treated like visiting royalty.

First of all, he organised a tea party for them, to which he also invited a few German women whom he thought might take a helpful interest in the newcomers. Next on his agenda were invitations to them to come in small groups for luxurious dinners that he had prepared for them as the resident chef. Ever mindful of their predicament, when he left Berlin to return home in haste, he thoughtfully bequeathed a ham to them, which would later become the highlight of their Christmas dinner.

Also among the first to take up the cause of entertaining 'the girls' were two American civilians, known only as Carl and Jerry, who initiated some of the more adventurous members of the *Damenstift* into the night life of wartime Berlin. They had all met at the regular Thursday night social gathering held by 'Uncle Stewart' at his church, and Carl and Jerry were quick to suggest the idea of going out to a pub for a glass or two of beer to finish off the evening. Vida, Olga and Jamie opted to return to the hotel, but Isabel, Kitsi and Doreen – whose fiancé was still forlornly waiting in South Africa – were game for a night on the town.

No dancing had been allowed publicly in Berlin since the beginning of casualties in Russia, but two pianos were tinkling forth mostly American dance music in that particular Ristorante Italiano. American music was forbidden even at that date – the end of September, 1941 – nevertheless, there it was, and we and many young officers of the Wehrmacht lapped up our beer to the swing accompaniment. It seemed odd to me that dancing was banned. Places like the Old Vaterland, for instance, down off the Potsdamer Platz, were crowded nightly with people like the young housekeepers from the Hotel Wartburg, our Hilde and Elsa and Erne and their soldier beaux. It seemed to me that the morale and health of the nation might have been better served by dancing rather than by just sitting sousing their youthful troubles in watery beer.[16]

The good times with Carl and Jerry turned out to be short-lived, however, when Carl left for the States in early October. Isabel, Kitsi and Doreen had joined the group of American wellwishers and diplomats who had gathered to see him off at the Anhalter Bahnhoff, and – by a stroke of luck – they were almost instantly taken in hand by Cyrus, a new face in the crowd, who immediately invited them to join him at his apartment for something to eat and drink. Isabel was especially delighted.

So we went home with Cyrus and that was our introduction to 12 Viktoriastrasse, which I shall remember all my life with greatest affection. For the next two months it was to be the setting for our nicest, coziest, funniest and most dramatic moments... Thin, nervous, and highly strung, he was on the verge of hysteria when we arrived on the scene. His life, for the past months, had been a series of too many climaxes – from getting his wife and children out of Norway after Germany had marched in, to rushing American Consulate personnel out of Germany the previous July. He had hidden newspaper men who knew too much from the Gestapo's eye; one of his greatest friends in Berlin was a Jew; he kept a Russian family from freezing and starvation...

We were only one of the near-lost causes he had worn himself to a frazzle over. But I will say this for us: I believe we saved his sanity during those last American months in Berlin. We were a breath of the free, still hopeful outside world – something which so many of the Americans left in Berlin at that time seemed to have forgotten existed. The poison of Europe, I think, had seeped into their veins. They had seen so much or heard so much at first hand that they were hardened to horror, and had become defeatist. We, who had ourselves come through the valley of the shadow, knew we had a world worthwhile returning to.

But the blackout curtains and heavy drapes of 12 Viktoriastrasse shut out the world of war on many happy evenings. There was that first one when Johanna, the phlegmatic German maid, was called in and instructed blithely by Cyrus to lay her cupboards bare for three hungry waifs who had emerged from the German storm. She showed no particular friendliness towards us – but many a good meal Hanni served us – and she even made a birthday cake for me with a hand-written card attached, expressing all the appropriate German sentiments on the occasion.

We shared Cyrus' air-raid cellar one night with Johanna and some of her friends. She seemed excited rather than resentful as our bombs came hurtling down. There were many German servants, I'm sure, serving good American masters, like Cyrus, who would have left with them if they could have. But Johanna had been to America once, with Cyrus' wife and children, and hadn't liked it much. She was German to the core...[17]

After this first successful meeting, there was a standing invitation to dinner and a bath at Viktoriastrasse every Friday night. Back at 'The Wart', the cost of a bath was two reichsmarks – a luxury the ladies could ill afford. This was money which could be better spent elsewhere, so with this in mind, the trio of Isabel, Kitsi and Doreen would look forward with delight to a wonderful supper and the comforting thought that they would be able to cleanse themselves of a week's grime on Bath Night. 'The Wart', by comparison, was drab, dirty and cramped, although its proprietors were surprisingly kind about housing these six women who – technically at least – were enemy aliens in their midst, any animosity they may have harboured against the six Canadians being well concealed.

Inevitably, as time went on, the rhythm of life for the inhabitants of the *Damenstift* assumed different patterns. Vida and Olga had established their supremacy as shoppers, whereas Isabel and Kitsi – by their own admission – were both still trying to figure out the significance of all the numbers on their food cards. Doreen and Jamie came in second on the shopping sweepstakes, leaving Isabel and Kitsi in their dust as they sallied forth each morning with their string shopping bags ready to forage for the best products available that day, before the supply dwindled to nothing. The other two 'incapables' found it impossible to compete, and returned home with such prizes as half a dozen lemons instead of the much-needed potatoes they should have purchased. In short, they were not cut out for the world of practicality. As a relative newcomer to married life, Kitsi had barely had an opportunity to begin running her own household, and Isabel's affluent background combined with her years in Rhodesia, where servants were always on hand to do her bidding, left both of them ill-equipped to make a significant contribution to either the acquisition of food or its preparation. Isabel's forays into the mysteries of where and how to buy alcoholic beverages were only slightly more successful, but her motivation to acquire these may have been greater.

And although 'The Incapables' – as the other members of the *Damenstift* had branded Kitsi and Isabel – may not have known much about shopping, let alone the joy of cooking, neither of them had any difficulty in meeting new people or making friends at a moment's notice. Both were quite capable of making the best of their bizarre situation as prisoners-at-large in Berlin, and often found themselves laughing in the face of adversity.

On Isabel's initiative, both she and Kitsi signed up for German lessons with Fräulein Schulze, a retired teacher who had been highly recommended to them. Twice a week, the two presented themselves at her door and she, in return, received five reichsmarks from each of her pupils. From their standpoint, this amount was far too little for what they received in return, although Isabel had difficulty in understanding this intelligent woman's misplaced loyalty to the Reich:

> Fräulein Schulze knew our circumstances – her great shining eyes welled with sympathy – and she would take no more. My conscience is partly salved by that fact that she was an idealist. She loved her Germany – it hurt her to admit its imperfections – and she, for one, would prove what a good German could be. Fräulein Schulze was, I would say, one of the few convinced Germans I met in Germany. She saw what good had come out of the Nazi regime, and would propound it, gently, but with the ardour of a firm believer…She had five nephews in the fighting ranks that winter. She lost pounds, which she couldn't spare, in worry over them – they were as close as sons to her, she would say – but she never criticised the reason why those beloved young nephews were sent to freeze their limbs or lives on the bitter Russian front.[18]

Isabel's comments reflect her genuine admiration for this generous and spirited woman, and is an indication of the feelings of mutual empathy and esteem that passed between them. To share rations or various tidbits with her from their Red Cross parcels seemed the least that she and Kitsi could do to ease the daily struggle for sustenance that was the lot of Germany's civilian population, including their warmhearted but underfed teacher.

True, there was often little enough for any of them to share. When the Canadians first arrived in Berlin, they were informed that since they now fell into the category of ex-internees, as such, they were no longer eligible to receive Red Cross parcels. It was largely due to the intervention of the medical director of the American embassy that their case was reviewed and an agreement made with an official of the British Red Cross in Geneva to ensure that they would receive parcels from time to time. Between 1939 and 1945, the estimated number of parcels distributed by the British Red Cross alone was estimated at over seventeen million, so it is not surprising that parcels periodically went astray or even went missing altogether.[19]

In the first weeks of their stay at 'The Wart', the Red Cross parcels addressed to the Hotel Wartburg arrived only infrequently, until it was discovered that for some unknown reason many of the packages originally meant for the Canadians had mistakenly been forwarded to the Egyptian crew of the *Zamzam* interned in one of the men's camps.

Once this came to light, all subsequent parcels were picked up in person at a customs depot, where the contents received a thorough examination before being released to the recipient. Kitsi later described her impressions of her encounters with the conscientious officials of the German customs department:

Each article, in turn, was inspected and weighed, but nothing was ever confiscated or declared dutiable. On one occasion I received a notice that a parcel had been sent to me through the Red Cross in England. It had been sent to Liebenau first and forwarded to Berlin. Inside were articles the Germans had not seen for years – white soap and toothpaste, a hairbrush, a fine woollen sweater and knitting wool – not to mention four large slabs of chocolate. The Customs man gazed at them woodenly – not quite believing his eyes, then called to some of his fellow-workers to inspect the parcel, too. Together they lifted each article, fingered it and smelled the soap and the real rubber in the hot-water bottle and pair of overshoes.

As the official had been very polite, I offered him a piece of chocolate, but he refused saying that he would have all those things when Germany had won the war. In fact, he didn't really sound too convinced.[20]

A changing of the guard

Several weeks after their release from internment in Liebenau, the Canadian inhabitants of the Hotel Wartburg received some unsettling news. It seemed that the authorisation which Herr Inspektor Thomma had written in their passports, leaving matters concerning their repatriation in the lap of the American embassy had been rejected on the grounds that this authorisation was not legitimate. According to the American diplomats, their situation – while regrettable – was such that it would require authorisation at the highest levels of government before they could be permitted to leave Berlin, and that, as a result, their stay there would have to be prolonged indefinitely – possibly even until the end of hostilities. The Canadians' naïve hopes of an early release had not taken into account the complicated bureaucratic negotiations that their status as civilians of a belligerent country would necessarily involve. Unfortunately, they would simply have to resign themselves to the fact that for the foreseeable future they would not be permitted to leave the city and that they would have to make the best of their predicament. It was an altogether gloomy prospect.

This new reality may well have been a contributing factor in Isabel and Kitsi's decision to begin learning German. Since they could well be in Berlin for an extended period, why not also set themselves up as highly qualified English teachers and put out feelers to see what might be waiting in the wings. Their monthly stipend of 150 reichsmarks per month was totally insufficient for their needs, and they welcomed with open arms the possibility of taking on their first pupil, whom they christened 'Line the Lovely'. They had met Line – the stunningly beautiful young German wife of a Finnish businessman, Teddy – through one of their military attaché contacts, and she had expressed an interest in learning 'American-English' and – until the Americans began leaving Berlin in droves – the arrangement proved mutually satisfactory. Isabel recalls these encounters with amusement:

> We would go at three o'clock in the afternoon to her stiffly modern German apartment. And sitting comfortably around her tiled coffee-table, we would feed her American slang while she fed us coffee and cakes and American cigarettes – the latter a gift from her military admirers. Line was smart and capable of great application, in the interests of romance and its by-products...
>
> It was thanks to Line and Teddy that we saw our one and only German fashion parade. Teddy was a wholesaler for women's clothing and took us one afternoon to his showroom, where we were among the fifty or so spectators of a rather sad affair. I wasn't expecting too much – since I've been told that even in peace time, the smart Berliner looks to Paris or Vienna for her styles – but the obvious lack of what contributes most to a successful fashion show was even greater than I had bargained for. And that was 'accessories'. The same hat appeared in unhappy combination with costumes for morning, pour le sport, or for a dressy afternoon. It was a large mustard-coloured flaring-brimmed sombrero and was worn by three of the four mannequins in turn. What passed for shoes were far from fashionable, and the effect of the one pair of stockings was not added to by a noticeably mended ladder...
>
> There was also a strangely noticeable lack of bosoms on show. It takes some degree of natural endowment to display any model to advantage. And four more flat-chested damsels I have seldom seen. No chests, no proper shoes, nor stockings. It seemed to me that those unfortunate models, running the gauntlet of our inspection on their oddly shod feet, expressed their embarrassment with every step, as if to say, 'Forgive us, we know what we do – but we can't help it.' Obviously Line didn't patronise her dear Teddy's lines of apparel, for her clothes were never anything but haute couture and her shoes and stockings not the style of Berlin 1941–42.[21]

Near the end of November, Teddy and Line left on a business trip to Vienna, with the promise that Line would call on their return and resume her lessons. However, there was never any further word from her. Once the United States had officially declared war on Germany, it seemed that the door had slammed shut on fraternisation with the Enemy. While the Americans were still in Berlin, the Canadians could pass as acceptable social contacts, but once that situation changed, in the estimation of many potential hosts and hostesses, Isabel and Kitsi quickly spiralled into the category of *persona non grata*.

Fortunately, in the meantime Isabel had taken on another pupil on a one-on-one basis. Almost on sight, the two women experienced an instant frisson of mutual admiration, and their relationship swiftly transcended the usual teacher–pupil formalities.

Lisbet, who had English and American friends, wanted to improve her knowledge of their language. Three mornings a week I would take a long ride and a long walk out to her Babelsberg home, and would arrive at her house chilled to the marrow by the bitter cold of Berlin's winter mornings after an insufficient breakfast. My appointed hour was eleven – whereupon Lisbet would rise from her downy couch and Gisella, the little maid, would bring a tray for both of us to the attractive living-room of her tastefully appointed apartment. Everything in that room was beautiful, rare and expensive. Lisbet's limousine sat somewhere in storage, its huge tires requisitioned by the Military. Her smaller car was loaned to an Embassy friend. No private citizen could drive a car. She played the Black Market for real coffee, and got it, however precariously! A bottle of French cognac would be produced on very cold mornings – a generous gesture to my frozen toes. It was always a present from a flier from Paris. Lisbet couldn't buy it. In fact, she could do almost none of the things she had been accustomed to doing. And that – to Lisbet – who had the wherewithal to indulge her slightest whim, was galling…

I can shed a tear or two for Lisbet – who was small and round, and gay and witty and wise…

Life may have been difficult for us orphans of the storm, stranded for a while on the enemy shore, but I felt infinitely sorrier for Lisbet because this was her country, though more by circumstance than by predilection, she being Viennese. Mainly she was flippant about the state of things in general, but I could never get her to elaborate. She would only shrug impatient shoulders and say, 'What can we do?' then switch to a current political joke – toilet paper – or the lack of it, which was a sore point in Germany about that time.[22]

Some of Lisbet's stories were untranslatable, but they proved to be an excellent vehicle for Isabel to learn some useful Berlin slang – something she would never have acquired in the course of her German lessons from Fräulein Schulze. One phrase of Lisbet's which Isabel found especially entertaining was the term 'Promenade Mischung' – the approximation in English of the word 'mongrel'. Along with the latest inside jokes, these words and phrases became a most useful addition to Isabel's Nazi-German vocabulary!

And while Isabel was learning the nuances of insider German, Olga, the idealist from the Canadian prairies, along with her fellow missionaries Vida and Jamie was making contacts of her own through attendance at various churches. Although the churches of many denominations had been closed, every Sunday, without fail, they would go either to the American or the Danish church and offer up their prayers – Vida and Jamie for their husbands languishing in a prisoner of war camp, Olga, who had left her heart in Africa, for her beloved mission in Natal. Through the good offices of Miss Wilhjelm of the YMCA, they also met once a week for bible study courses at the YWCA, where four of the former internees from Liebenau alternated in teaching classes.

Now and then they also found themselves witnessing events unfolding around them that were meant to stir the minds and hearts of the German *Volk*.

We saw our first big Nazi demonstration on 25 November when Berlin crowds gathered to pay final homage to Werner Mölders, a hero of the German Luftwaffe, who had been killed in an accident in Germany after taking part in over a hundred 'dogfights'. Over one thousand soldiers took part in the procession and Goering, the head of the Luftwaffe, and Foreign Minister von Ribbentrop accompanied the body. The coffin, draped with the Swastika, was preceded by a massive display of tanks and gun carriages as crowds formed along the route.

Late one evening as we walked down the street, we noticed a crowd gathering in front of one of the big concert halls. We pressed our way to the curb just in time to see Goebbels come out of the building and enter a waiting car. The crowd stiffened their arms in a salute and cheered frantically before moving off into the Berlin night.[23]

Olga also describes the throngs of people who congregated in front of Hitler's Berlin residence in hopes of catching a glimpse of 'Der Führer'. Even the knowledge of his presence inside the house seemed to hold the people gathered there under a sort of hypnotic power. The mere sight of his car incited wild cheering, saluting and the metallic click of soldiers' boots, but all was not quite what it seemed.

From Olga's standpoint, the cheering was a form of release and compensation for weeks and months of suppressed whispers. In a crowd, people could raise their voices without the fear of their private remarks being overheard by the omnipresent listeners of the Gestapo or the SS. In one grand outburst, Berliners shouted before settling back into the oppressive silence of those who dared not speak. On the other hand, they swarmed into the opera houses and concert halls to listen. And tickets for any performance were sold out almost before they'd been issued to the vendors. With a system which reserved 75 per cent of the tickets to any concert for the military, it was next to impossible to obtain a seat of any kind out of the 25 per cent which went on sale to the general public. But there was always the chance of hitting the jackpot, which helps to explain the length of the queues in front of box offices on any day of the week.

One of Isabel's personal coups was managing to get tickets to hear two concerts of the Berlin Philharmonic under the baton of the renowned conductor-composer Wilhelm Furtwängler. But if tickets for the Philharmonic were difficult to come by, obtaining tickets for any of Berlin's three opera houses was an even greater challenge – and a more expensive one too. After lining up several times from eight in the morning till noon to try to get a cheap seat, Isabel finally decided to part with a good portion of her monthly allowance and indulge herself in a front-row seat for a performance of Wagner's *Tristan and Isolde*.

Olga, who was also a serious music-lover, made the observation that it was virtually impossible to satisfy Berlin audiences.

> Grasping at the release which accompanied the experience, they demanded encore after encore. With insatiable appetites, their applause beckoned back the performers; and even after the last note had been played and the concert ended, they thronged the stage requesting more. Berlin's hunger for good music grew increasingly as all other avenues of escape were cut off.[24]

Yet another refuge from earthly cares could be found in Berlin's places of worship. Olga notes that by the time she arrived there in the early autumn of 1941, most of the pastors had already been taken away – either to prison camps or for service in the military. Only a few were permitted to remain and carry on their work with ever-expanding congregations. Sunday schools were depleted since the children of Party officials were forbidden to attend and the rest were discouraged from participation. The Hitler Youth movement held them firmly in its grasp.

On the outskirts of Berlin, the church of the renowned poet and anti-Nazi activist Pastor Martin Niemöller was still open for worship, although Niemöller had long since been incarcerated. Even today, the final words of Niemöller's best-known poem continue to resonate throughout the world: 'They came for me and there was no one left to speak out for me.' Each evening at sunset intercessory services were held for all the pastors confined in Germany's prisons and concentration camps. Olga records her impressions:

> One night we attended the service and heard a list of twenty-nine names read off, with Niemöller's name heading the list. Niemöller,

himself, was still in a concentration camp and his wife was only allowed to see him for fifteen minutes every two weeks. Inquiring about the possibility of his release, we received the reply, 'Never, as long as Hitler is in power'... At this stage, most of the church bells had been confiscated to be melted down into munitions. All sermons were written out and submitted for censorship by Nazi officials before being preached. No Christian literature could be printed or mimeographed. Everything had to be written by hand or on a typewriter. The worshippers brought their own hymn books to church with them and those who had none soon learned to memorise the words.[25]

And finally on 8 December the American church was closed, the last sermon delivered on 7 December before news of the Japanese attack on Pearl Harbor had reached Germany. For the Canadians, the US declaration of war spelled the end of any remaining hope they might have had of an imminent release. Instead, it was the beginning of a lengthy period of marking time over a long, harsh winter. From now on – aside from the interventions of their Danish guardian angel – they would be on their own.

From Isabel's perspective, the last desperate days of the Americans' departure from Berlin were filled with almost incredible stress and anxiety.

I remember, on the Tuesday following the fateful Sunday of Japan's attack, wondering if I should venture out to my lesson with Lisbet in Babelsberg, so far away from the protective Embassy. Anything could happen at any moment, and I, for one, didn't want to be out there alone in Berlin when it did. I asked Cyrus whether I should risk it and he said, 'Yes, go, but telephone me while you're there.'

That morning Lisbet was as tense as I was. She had good friends among the Americans, too, and didn't want to see them go. We talked of nothing but the pros and cons of America's entering the War. We played some Bach records, to steady our nerves and smoked many too many of Lisbet's rationed cigarettes. At last I could stand it no longer, and telephoned Cyrus.

'Where are you?' he demanded, 'You must come right here, as soon as you can.'

Lisbet practically pushed me out the door. That journey back to town was one of the longest half-hours I've ever known. From the Potsdamer Platz I walked, then half-ran up Hermann Goering Strasse to the Embassy. It was windy and the last leaves from the trees in the Tiergarten were blowing forlornly in haphazard flurries, across the wide street.

Cyrus was alone in his office when Isabel arrived. She knew immediately that the situation was serious when he grabbed her by the shoulders, drew her to him and kissed her. He told her that he had spent the entire morning burning papers and that they'd made an enormous bonfire of them in the embassy's basement. Now it would only be a matter of time before he and the other diplomats would be picked up, so why not have a last fling at his apartment on Viktoriastrasse? Besides, he didn't want to be alone. Isabel must bring over 'the girls' to make a celebratory night of it. And they must also be there to hear Roosevelt's speech at five o'clock the next morning, so they should pack an overnight bag.

Viktoriastrasse was festive that night. Cyrus was in top gear – his characteristic reaction to excitement and everyone responded. Glen, a United Press correspondent, was there and Pat, the other United Press man, came in after a while with startling news. All the German newsmen had been picked up in the USA. 'Why in hell did they have to do that?' Glen groaned. 'Now it will be our turn next. No question about it!'

Dinner was lavish. A lot of American canned goods were opened since the boys didn't expect to need them much longer. By midnight, everybody was pretty well exhausted. Cyrus ordered us all to bed, or to rest – to be awakened at five for the President's speech. Sensibly Doreen and Jamie went right to bed and I think they actually slept. I took off my shoes and stretched out on the living-room couch but couldn't sleep. Soon it was five o'clock, but the speech turned into a fiasco. Static intervened and we could hear nothing more than the faint familiar timbre of the President's voice.

Johanna appeared about seven, looked a little startled at the various recumbent forms strewn about the living room, but went quietly ahead setting the table for breakfast. In various stages of disrepair we sat down to breakfast. There was a knock at the front door. We heard Johanna go and, in the silence which had automatically fallen upon us, we heard her say, 'Heil Hitler.'

'That's for us, Pat,' said Glen, and got up from the table. But Cyrus shoved him back in his seat. 'Don't anybody move. Don't speak,' he said, in a stern whisper. 'I'll go to the door. This is my house. This is still American territory. They can't touch you here.' Before he reached the door, we heard it close. Cyrus came back with the report from Johanna that the early-morning caller had been one of the Schutz Polizei, checking to see if two United Press correspondents really lived at this address, as listed.

Glen got up from the table, went into the living room and returned with a small American flag which Cyrus had had flying from his desk since Sunday night. He stood it in a glass. 'Good old Stars and Stripes forever.' He said it jauntily enough, but the hand that pushed the glass to the centre of the breakfast table was just a little shaky, I noticed...Cyrus took the situation in hand. Glen was to go out first, alone. He wanted to report to the office. When – and if – he got there, he would then telephone Pat since there was no use in both of them getting picked up together. I had an appointment at the Embassy that morning, so I was allowed to go second. Also alone. The other girls were to leave in pairs, at well-spaced intervals.

So that was Tuesday night. A night, or nightmare, which extended itself as a prolonged suspense through the next four days, till Saturday, when the Embassy people and newspapermen received the order that they had been waiting for. They were to be ready for temporary internment in the spa hotel of Bad Nauheim.

Kitsi and I spent that last night at Viktoriastrasse. The Press boys had been picked up and jailed on the Thursday, but were set free on Saturday night to make ready for departure with the diplomats on Sunday. None of us slept, or even tried to...We sat amidst the wreck of the half-dismantled apartment, and drank the last gallons of Cyrus' tea, and talked about our possible futures. Kitsi and I didn't want to think about ours very much. The boys were quite disconnected. Glad that it had really happened at last...after the past months of uncertainty.

'If only the *Zamzam* girls could come with us, I'd cry for joy,'
Cyrus said, for the ninety-ninth time. But we couldn't. So about
eight o'clock on Sunday morning, after Johanna had brewed us
coffee which none of us could drink, we all walked through the
Tiergarten together and said good-bye by Goethe's statue. Then
Kitsi and I went back one final time to Viktoriastrasse, to collect
the things the boys had left for us: food, of course, Glen's tennis
racquet, Cyrus's cosy flannelette nightgown, and an unabridged
edition of *Mein Kampf*. We said good-bye to Johanna and went
sadly home to 'the Wart'. It was Sunday morning. The streets
were deserted, and there was a fine drizzle of rain.[26]

Christmas in Germany

As the dark days of December descended on them, there were
also changes taking place at the Hotel Wartburg. Olga and
Vida had decided that their life of relative isolation might be
improved upon if they moved over to the hospice on Linkstrasse
to join their former Liebenau friends already ensconced there.
Dispirited by the departure of the Americans and their dealings
with the less approachable Swiss who had taken over the
Canadian file, Jamie and Doreen had resorted to doing little
beyond eating, sleeping and walking over to the hospice to visit
Vida, Olga and the others from Liebenau.

At this point there were close to twenty women from
Liebenau, varying in age from 14 to 70, scattered about in the
cheap and cheerless hostelries of Berlin. Perhaps this is what
prompted some thoughtful soul in the German bureaucracy to
seize upon the idea that perhaps 19 women should have some
sort of male escort. In this case it turned out to be the 75-year-
old husband of the eldest of the women in the hospice, who was
released from his internment camp to join his wife. They were
an exceptionally warm and likeable couple, who insisted on
Christian names – Ettie and Dudley – and so they were known
from that day forward.

Just a few days before Christmas, Kitsi and Isabel – both feeling particularly downhearted and homesick – decided to take an early evening jaunt. Some fresh air and exercise was just what the doctor ordered to banish the pre-Christmas blues. Through the crowds they made their way up the Wilhelmstrasse, past the great cold façade of the Air Ministry, past the Wilhelmplatz and under the small famous balcony from which so many inflammatory speeches had been delivered, then past the Führer's residence with its square front garden of potted plants always in bloom…And from there it was on to Unter den Linden, where they turned left in the direction of a small stationery shop where they hoped they might be able to find a few Christmas cards. But they were out of luck. Not a card to be seen. All sold out, much like almost everything else on the Berlin market. Next to the stationer's was a large florist filled to overflowing with exotic blooms – orchids, bougainvilleas, poinsettias, cyclamen and fuchsia – all hopelessly out of their price range.

It was at this point that they suddenly struck upon the idea of sipping a cheering cocktail at the exclusive Adlon Hotel just next door. What better way to brighten their sagging spirits? The Adlon was well known as a personal favourite of the members of the upper echelons of the Nazi Party. In fact, word even had it that the Führer himself frequented it from time to time. It was also the temporary home of the famous British writer and humourist Pelham Grenville Wodehouse, more popularly known as P.G. The author of dozens of widely read books, Wodehouse enjoyed a huge following in the United States as well as in his native Britain. In late 1934, he had made the decision to move to France, where he remained until it was too late to avoid arrest by the invading German army in 1940. After a stint in a POW camp in Belgium, he was interned at Tost in Upper Silesia, and in the autumn of 1941 was relocated to Berlin to begin a series of broadcasts aimed specifically at listeners in the United States. To the majority of the British public, this was nothing short of treachery, and the name Wodehouse became the centre of a controversy that has quietly reverberated through the intervening years. Those speaking in his defence have claimed that the Germans successfully manipulated him into an untenable position by taking advantage of his political naïveté, whereas his detractors considered him a shameless traitor.[27]

And it is at this point that Isabel takes up the tale of her Adlon adventure with Kitsi:

> And it was as we were going through the portals of Berlin's most expensive hotel that we suddenly thought: 'Isn't P. G. Wodehouse supposed to live here? Perhaps he, too, is feeling a little low over America's entry into the War. He might even be glad to see us. Let's call on him.' It was an impulse of the moment. We had heard from some of the Americans that his name was an abomination to any right-thinking American and to the British in general, because he was believed to have been released from a German internment camp by agreeing to broadcast over the Nazi radio. But at that moment we weren't thinking whether this judgment was right or wrong. We were simply feeling that here was someone British – the creator of something as delightfully British as Bertie Wooster and Mr Jeeves – alone and surrounded by a hostile world.
>
> So in we went and up to the reception desk... Yes, Mr and Mrs Wodehouse were guests there and their room number was such and such. Would we like to go up? That rather took our breath away. We hadn't expected a 'Mrs Wodehouse'. It's always a little easier to foist yourself upon a strange man than on a strange woman and also, it did seem a little brazen to knock on Fame's door unannounced. We temporised by asking the clerk to telephone their room, wondering just what we would say to introduce ourselves. When he said that their rooms gave no answer, it was almost a relief. We beat a retreat to the lounge, saying we would try again later.

A young Italian waiter came to take their order, and by the time he had returned with it their courage was already on the rise. Did he know the Wodehouses, they inquired. Oh yes, came the reply and he then proceeded to tell them that the great man generally came in about this time. 'He takes his dog for a walk every afternoon. You watch out for a man with a little dog – you'll see him coming through any time now.'

> So we watched and waited, but he didn't come. The waiter flitted by every once in a while to ask if we had seen him. By this time, he seemed much more anxious for the meeting than were we. We ordered a second drink. Cocktails, even poor as they were, with a base of some synthetic gin, were expensive – but we were in a mood for desperate extravagance that evening. When the waiter returned with our drinks, he asked if we would like to meet Herr Plack. 'He's the Foreign Office man who looks after the Wodehouses,' he told us, 'and he's in the lobby now.'

Kitsi and Isabel assented, though not with any great enthusiasm, and the waiter rushed off. In a few minutes he arrived back on the scene with Herr Plack – a pleasant-mannered young German with a noticeably broken nose. Over cocktails, he later revealed that this had occurred during a visit to Hollywood where, some time in the autumn of 1939, a certain famous personality had thrown something hard at him and called him a 'dirty Nazi'. In the best interests of his future, Max Plack had decided it might be best to withdraw from the American scene for a while, although he seemed to harbour no particular resentment against the lady in question. His present assignment seemed to be, as the waiter had said, to look after the Wodehouses, and after listening to an abridged version of Kitsi and Isabel's Berlin predicament, he assured them that he was quite certain Mr Wodehouse would be interested in meeting them. With that, he went off to telephone the Great One while Isabel looked at Kitsi, wondering if she were dreaming all of this. But no – Herr Plack was back in no time with the news that Mr Wodehouse was just finishing shaving and that he and Mrs Wodehouse would be down shortly to join them.

> They came. We were introduced and Mr Wodehouse registered surprise: Herr Plack's message, as he had heard it, was that 'two

comedians were waiting below to see him.' Mr Plack's English was excellent, but perhaps the telephone wires may have transmitted 'Canadians' as 'comedians'. Or perhaps 'P.G.', like us, felt badly in need of some comic relief, as he quipped that it must have been 'wishful hearing'. At any rate, it was the one witty remark I heard him make.

We all sat down and had a drink together and the Wodehouses invited Kitsi and me to have dinner with them. During the course of the considerable time we spent in his company, Wodehouse's conversation seemed that of a thoroughly bewildered man. His attitude concerning the stand the British public was taking against him, was not one of injury exactly. He seemed simply not to understand. I have no idea whether his lack of comprehension was deliberately stupid or merely the vagary of a perhaps impractical turn of mind. I can only say that it seemed genuine. He had been released from internment, he told us, because of his advanced age. He may even have believed this and went on to say that in his radio talks he had only wanted to be a bit silly about what it felt like to be interned. He hadn't even thought about the propaganda angle. I guess he expected his own country to recognise the old Wodehousian touch.

Mrs Wodehouse's worries were more on the practical side. Her daily routine (in bed till noon, then lunch, followed by a walk with the dog (a Pekinese) in the Tiergarten, dinner, then bed again) didn't much amuse her. She disliked the food, both for themselves and their little dog. She wrapped up the grisly scraps from our dinner plates in a napkin to take to her poor pet! She hated Berlin's cold. And she was worried about money. Were we able to get money from America, she asked ingenuously? Which was an interesting sidelight, as some of the criticism of 'Plum' and Ethel Wodehouse – the P.G.s – had arisen from their staying in one of Berlin's most expensive hotels. Where did they get the money? Well, if the Nazis had given them a permanent rain check on the Adlon, Mrs Wodehouse didn't seem to know it.

That was the last Kitsi and Isabel saw of P.G., although they were later asked to attend a tea party to which both Wodehouses had also been invited. Only Ethel turned up, because her dearest Plum was feverishly finishing off the last chapters of a book which he hoped to send to America with the returning diplomats and journalists. Harry Flannery, the American CBS broadcaster who would later write *Assignment to Berlin*, is reputed to have told Wodehouse, when asked if he thought the new book would sell in the States, 'Not if you continue to broadcast over the Nazi radio.'[28] In total, Wodehouse recorded only five radio broadcasts, and the jury remains out on whether this was actively unpatriotic or just a practical response to his circumstances.

In any case, Isabel chose to give Wodehouse the benefit of the doubt.

> I believe, however, that I can vouch for Ethel Wodehouse's unmixed feelings. Almost her first question to me at a mutual friend's tea-party was: 'How are you getting along with your study of German?' I said I wasn't yet exactly fluent. How about her progress? Oh, she hadn't learned a word. The German language was quite beyond her…always had been…always would be. Apparently she was right.
>
> It seemed incredible but, when – a little later – a German-speaking guest greeted another with the usual 'Guten Tag', Mrs P.G. leaned across the tea-table to me and asked: 'Guten Tag'… what does that mean? I hear it so often.' I can't believe she is truly quite that stupid, so surely her apparent impregnability to a language being spoken on all sides of her for many, many months must have been deliberate.[29]

The Adlon encounter was not the only highlight of the otherwise gloomy month of December 1941. To help lift the pervasive gloom that had begun to settle in, the idea of a *Damenstift* Christmas dinner at 'the Wart' became a welcome prospect. Close to eight months had passed since the sinking of the *Zamzam*, and the date of the Canadians' anticipated departure from Berlin now seemed further away than ever. It was high time to haul out 'Uncle' Stewart's ham and the canned goods they'd received from Betty, the departing wife of an American diplomat, and have themselves a celebratory feast. Isabel captures the spirit of the moment in her depiction of the elaborate preparations for this grand occasion:

Frau Meier, the Wart's proprietress, was approached, and generously contributed the Wart's kitchen and dining-room and facilities. Fortune favoured us, too, in that travel was made difficult for Germans over the holiday season, so that the hotel was almost empty except for us, its permanent guests. Vida took charge, of course, with Doreen an able second-in-command. I was permitted to decorate. A table for twenty allows some scope. Berlin shop windows were gaily decorated for Christmas, although inside there was little to buy, and we had no money for Christmas frills anyway. Luckily, the Potsdamerstrasse flower stalls were well stocked with scented boughs of evergreen – for the Wart's table linen needed some masking. In Berlin's Woolworths were bright-coloured balls for the price of a few pfennigs. In another store I came upon cunning little wooden candelabra, but without any candles. Providentially, Miss Wilhjelm provided these, purchased with this very occasion in mind on her last trip to Switzerland.

All in all, it was a scene such as 'the Wart' had never seen before, nor probably will again. Frau Meier's eyes opened wider and wider as she watched the progress of preparations. And when we all sat down – with Dudley, our one man, at the head of the long *Damenstift* table – looking for all the world like Father Christmas with his pink cheeks, blue eyes and snow-white hair – skillfully attacking not only the ham but a whole leg of lamb for which the twenty of us had contributed our meat tickets, poor Frau Meier shook her poor old head and sighed deeply. She hadn't seen so much meat on one table at one time in many a moon. She went away muttering, 'Zu viel, zu viel.' But I don't believe she really thought it was too much when later we prevailed upon her to take enough of it to give herself and the shy Herr Meier the first square meat-based meal they had probably had in a couple of years. Poor Frau Meier – with her only son in Russia, it wasn't much of a Christmas for her.[30]

For two of the participants, this joyful Christmas Day celebration had been preceded by another equally memorable occasion. Through their American friend Cyrus, just a month after their arrival, 'the girls' had made the acquaintance of an elderly Jewish professor, whom Cyrus described as the embodiment of a fast-disappearing species – a living, breathing example of *Altberliner Kultur*. The Professor described himself as very deaf, blind in one eye and visually identifiable due to the obligatory yellow star he wore as a sign that his presence in Germany was no longer welcome. His finely drawn features, his sense of humour, his incisive wit, and extraordinary zest for life combined to endear him instantly to all who entered his sphere. For Isabel it had been love at first sight.

It quickly became obvious that their admiration was mutual, and on each occasion that they met the pleasure derived from their new-found friendship warmed them both. With the departure of Isabel's American friends and the approach of Christmas, the Professor's invitation to join him for dinner on Christmas Eve at his magnificent old home on the shores of the Wannsee was an indication of how greatly he valued the bond that had developed between them. Doreen Turner, the young Canadian bride-to-be, had agreed to keep Isabel company, and together she and Isabel were entertained in grand style, beginning with tea and a delectable home-baked *Stollen*. Afterwards, together with the Professor, they leafed through the pages of many of his old family albums, enjoying the highlights of his long and colourful life. Then came the long-awaited moment when the dining-room door was thrown open, and there before them was the setting for their first and last celebration of a traditional Christmas Eve in Germany.

A blue spruce had blown down in his garden the week before and now became the perfect Christmas tree. From its branches grew dozens of pure white candles. Only the candles adorned that perfect tree. Anything more would have been artistic imperfection. To one side of its base was the scene of the manger and the white glow of the many candles cast a pure heavenly light on the faces of the Shepherds and Wise Men from the East in their richly coloured robes...

Then came the dinner – a rich, fat, juicy duck – roasted to a perfect crispness. A finer bird could not have appeared on the table of the Dictator of the fate of the Jews. And, as a finishing touch, the Professor produced two bottles of French red wine for his guests. The aftermath of that dinner I can't quite remember. I expect our unaccustomed stomachs were too gorged to allow our minds to register. But I do remember the walk back along the lake, through a night whose sky was intensely brilliant with stars and a moon and the criss-crossing beams of the powerful Berlin searchlights…

Doreen and I said little to one another. Our hearts were a little too full for many words to be spoken. It was the Midnight Eve – our Christmas well begun with the hospitality of heart and hearth – from a Jew to two Canadians in Germany.[31]

And the next night, when they celebrated their own Christmas with all the members of the *Zamzam* group, at one point Doreen and Isabel caught each other's eyes and drank a silent toast to the lonely old Professor, whose family had long since left the country. Only the Professor had chosen to stay on and live out what little time was left to him in his beloved German Fatherland.

In the heart of the Third Reich

With Christmas behind them, in the cold winter months ahead food grew rapidly poorer and scarcer, and there was no more Chianti – even for privileged patrons of the local Italian restaurant. And, as the war news grew better for the Allies and worse for Germany, the *Sondermeldung* or *Special News Bulletin* would blare forth with the volume turned up, yet no one stopped eating and talking. Nor did they listen. They had long since tuned out.

Eventually most of the original *Damenstift* group gave up restaurants altogether and prepared their own meals at 'the Wart'. But neither Kitsi nor Isabel was very adept at turning out anything noticeably appetising and, as a result, they resorted to the occasional meal at a local eatery. It couldn't be much worse than their own cooking, and besides it gave them an opportunity to mingle with others and feel the pulse of the public morale.

At this point, a decree had been issued that military personnel were to be served first, however – not surprisingly – this new regulation was met with little enthusiasm on the part of the increasingly disgruntled civilian patrons, whose patience had already been sorely tried.

The people of Berlin were beginning to show signs of the toll the war was taking on them, but great pains were also being taken to conceal the city's visible scars from its citizens. Scaffolding had been erected around buildings – such as the opera house – which had suffered serious damage from bombing attacks. Other destruction had been completely concealed by high wooden fences. As a precautionary measure, the entire length of Unter den Linden from the Zoo to the Brandenburg Gate had been reduced to single-lane traffic in order that a green canopy could be raised to cover the other half of the avenue and render it less distinguishable to Allied aircraft.

As early as the end of 1940, fairly extensive attempts at camouflage had already been undertaken to disguise the 8 km East–West corridor of the city as well as surrounding areas such as the Lietzensee in Charlottenburg.[32] These efforts at concealment involved not only specific landmarks and buildings that could be distinguished from above, but they also applied to all ground transportation. Streetcars were blacked out after dark so that the only visible lights in the city were the searchlight beams criss-crossing in mid-air in search of 'enemy' aircraft. Olga observed in her notebook that on clear nights it was possible for the Canadians to count as many as forty or fifty beams playing across the sky, picking up the swarm of German fighter planes that were conducting anti-aircraft manoeuvres above them. Until now, the heaviest Allied raids had mainly been concentrated on the port cities of the north and in the industrial Ruhr Valley; however, there was no guarantee that Berlin would be spared from heavy bombing for much longer. It was best to be prepared for the worst and adopt all possible measures to ensure the relative safety of the city's population. Among these, the obvious need to build more and larger bunkers became a top priority. Each night children from the outlying districts were bussed into the city and herded into the bowels of a vast air-raid shelter in the centre of the city.

From Olga's perspective, however, it was the people themselves who best displayed what Berlin attempted to hide. And this applied particularly to a segment of the population that reflected the most reprehensible aspect of life in Nazi Germany – the Jews of Berlin – moving furtively into the stores during the last shopping hour – between five and six – to buy their significantly smaller allotment of food. All known Jews had been issued special ration cards – marked with the letter 'J' – to ensure that the rules were strictly applied. Large areas of the city were declared off-limits, and the yellow-star laws had long since been enacted. Banned from entering certain districts and from any stores displaying 'Jews and dogs forbidden' signs, many roamed the back streets aimlessly or huddled on their specially designated yellow park benches listlessly awaiting their turn to be picked up for 'relocation'. By June 1943, an official proclamation was made that Berlin was – to all intents and purposes – a city without Jews. In a decade under the yoke of Adolf Hitler's regime, the capital's original Jewish population of a hundred and sixty thousand in 1933 had been reduced to those who remained either undeclared or in hiding. In Olga's words,

> During the winter of 1941 we had seen many Jews in the Berlin streets, shoveling snow from the snowdrifts left after a heavy winter storm. But now there were fewer and fewer of them. They were gradually being replaced by the equally despised Poles... Even in the early Spring of 1942 we could notice a lessening in their numbers, for Hitler intended to make good on his promise. Those who had not obtained entry to another country or found release by using the gas range on their own stoves must still be removed from Germany by the end of 1943. And as legal means failed, other methods were resorted to throughout Germany.

The methods of relocation were not uniform but through the grapevine, the stories of Jewish disposals had spread throughout Germany. And like all others who lived within the confines of Berlin we, too, knew the meaning of that familiar phrase, 'Another Jew is missing.'[33]

As an illustration of the implementation of this well-orchestrated removal policy, Olga tells the story of an elderly Jewish man known to her and her fellow missionaries who was commanded to relinquish his seat in the streetcar by a member of the ever-present Gestapo. Being well over eighty, the man was rather slow in complying – much to the annoyance of the impatient Gestapo agent, who ordered him to produce his identity papers. After submitting his papers for inspection, he was told to report to the police station the following day, and once he had crossed the threshold there was no further word of him. Nor did anyone dare to inquire.

The citizens of Germany had become well schooled in the dangers implicit in being too friendly with Jews. One young German, in compliance with Nazi regulations, had set out to visit the special bureau where he could apply for permission to marry a girl who was known to the officials as one of the many Germans whose ancestry revealed a trace of Jewish blood. This meant that his bride-to-be was on record as a second-class citizen, unsuitable for marriage to a German with a pedigree of racial purity. Once again, the story ended within the walls of officialdom. The young man never reappeared.

Olga went on to outline her own impressions of the accelerated deportation process as it applied to the Jews of Berlin. Her personal horror is very much in evidence as she writes,

All over Germany, they disappeared – sometimes singly, sometimes in large numbers. Many of them had been herded together and sent into occupied Poland. Usually they were taken from their homes at night. While Berlin slept, the Gestapo made the rounds of Jewish homes. On ten minutes' notice they would be taken to the small railroad station for shipment to Poland. One such group, huddled together in the bitter cold of a Berlin winter night, was standing on a platform waiting for the train when the guards went through the entire group snipping away the fur collars from their coats.[34]

Absolutely nothing must go to waste. With the Russian campaign going from bad to worse, Germany's soldiers were clamouring for any scraps of fur or wool for mittens and scarves that could help protect them from the unbearable cold. And the citizens of Berlin, already hard-pressed by the demands of the war effort, were constantly being met on the streets by uniformed fundraisers exhorting passers-by to make contributions towards 'winter relief for the poor'. These demands were met with more than a little cynicism on the part of anyone unlucky enough to be accosted, since it was common knowledge that the accumulated offerings were simply added to the coffers of the Nazi Party for war-related expenditure. Certainly not for the poor.

In fact, many a Berliner was provided with a good chuckle at the expense of these 'winter relief' fundraisers when an apocryphal story was widely circulated to the effect that the local people in Scotland had all taken to their heels and fled to the woods after Rudolph Hess landed his aircraft in their midst in 1941. Surely anyone with any sense at all would know that the real reason for his arrival there was to collect for 'winter relief'![35]

By the same token, in the eyes of the ruling elite the less Germany's people knew of the horrific conditions at the front the better. To counteract any possible doubt about Germany's invincibility in the war against the Soviets, Propaganda Minister Goebbels struck upon an ideal solution. An enormous exhibition hall would be constructed in the heart of downtown Berlin. The site was within a few blocks of the Wartburg Hotel, so the Canadians were ideally situated to watch Herr Goebbels's brainchild being erected. Its purpose would be to display to the German public elaborate scenes of the horrors of life in Communist Russia and the uncivilised conditions that prevailed there. Surely this would come as a shot in the arm to those who might have lost some of their enthusiasm for the war on the Eastern Front.

After it was opened to the public early in May 1942, Berlin's schoolchildren and others from the outlying districts were brought in for special tours of Goebbels's pet project. The following month a fire broke out in the main building, and the usual suspects – two hundred of Berlin's dwindling Jewish population – were rounded up and a number of them were executed in reprisal. As long as Hitler remained in power, there was little hope for the Jews remaining in Berlin.

There were, however, a few notable exceptions to the routine victimisation that came as a result of Jewish ancestry, and among these was Bernhard Rogge. Although it is highly doubtful that the women of the *Zamzam* who were left marking time in Hitler's stronghold were remotely aware of his presence in Berlin early in January 1942, Rogge and the crew of the *Atlantis* had been transported there by special train to receive a heroes' welcome.

Rogge's friend and benefactor, Rear-Admiral Erich Räder, was waiting to greet and decorate each man in turn at a specially planned ceremony. Rogge had also been singled out for promotion to Admiral, and became the recipient of an additional honour. His original First World War Iron Cross would be supplemented by one of the Third Reich's most highly prized decorations, the Knight's Cross.

After the sinking of the *Zamzam*, the *Atlantis* had continued to fulfil its allotted mission for another six months, and had either seized or sunk a handful of Allied merchant ships, before becoming the target of a surprise attack on 22 November 1941 in the vicinity of Ascension Island. To the captain of the British battlecruiser HMS *Devonshire*, the silhouette of the *Atlantis* was instantly recognisable thanks to David Scherman's *Life* magazine photograph, which had been posted in the officers' ward room of every British ship-of-the-line six months earlier. The fabled 'profile shot' that Scherman had risked from the vantage point of his lifeboat as it rowed away from the sinking *Zamzam* was about to decide the fate of the legendary German raider. Like so many of her own victims, the *Atlantis* had become the proverbial sitting duck.

Within minutes, eight well-placed shells from the *Devonshire* had inflicted serious damage. Fires were breaking out faster than they could be extinguished, and it was clear to Rogge that the time had come to begin lowering the boats and set the charges for scuttling the ship. Typically, Rogge himself remained reluctant to leave the bridge, and was only persuaded to go over the side at the last possible moment. The unforeseen end of the *Atlantis* had taken less than two hours, and the *Devonshire* had already steamed out of sight.

Then, like a mirage, the bow of the U-124 broke the surface and the lengthy process of taking the wounded on board and stringing out the lifeboats for a massive towing operation began. A regular routine of eight-hour shifts was devised whereby one-third of the survivors were crammed into the U-boat, another third sat in the dinghies lashed to the submarine's deck, and the remainder braved the elements in the boats towed in its wake. Four weeks and eight thousand kilometres later, Captain Rogge and his crew arrived in the port of St Nazaire in Brittany.

News of their safe return and near-miraculous survival was heralded as a heroic triumph for the Reich, and generated the Berlin ceremony held in their honour. Having survived the harrowing and hazardous journey back to Occupied France, Rogge and his men had briefly become celebrities. But Germany was at war, and their moment of glory was necessarily fleeting. After being granted two months' leave, the former crew members of the *Atlantis* were each assigned to new duties in the service of their country, and went their separate ways. Many would not live to witness Germany's defeat.

Among these was Bernhard Rogge's highly esteemed young gunnery officer, First Lieutenant Lorenz Kasch, who had served all 655 days on board the *Atlantis* with him. Kasch had made the fateful decision – in the face of all advice to the contrary – to volunteer for U-boat duty in the hope of obtaining the Führer's personal permission to marry one of the Reich's second-class citizens. By virtue of her Jewish grandmother, his fiancée was deemed unsuitable for marriage to an officer of Hitler's Kriegsmarine, and Kasch would have to prove himself worthy of becoming an exception. With the odds for survival distinctly stacked against him, Kasch's dreams for the future were never fulfilled. He went missing in October 1943 on his first tour of duty as the captain of a U-540.

Several years later, as part of a post-war attempt to compensate for past wrongs, Kasch's grieving fiancée was offered the possibility of participation in a posthumous marriage. To honour his devotion to her, she accepted and – accompanied by her father – she was duly joined in matrimony in a civil ceremony with Lorenz Kasch's officer's cap, placed on a chair beside her as mute testimony of his absence.

The winter of 1941–42 found Kathleen Levitt and her children still in the relative safety of Liebenau, untouched by the war and no longer under suspicion of being Jewish. Time and again, she would think back to her sudden impulse to dispose of her incriminating passport when the *Zamzam* came under attack, and thank her lucky stars. From the contents of the letters she received at regular intervals from Kitsi and Isabel in Berlin, she was also reassured that the decision she had made to remain with Peter and Wendy in Liebenau had been for the best. The high hopes of her friends for an early release and a speedy return to Canada appeared to be stalled indefinitely.[36] And to make matters worse, they were now living in constant fear of the Allied air raids. To compound the situation, the frequency of the raids had somewhat intensified – but only slightly in comparison to what was happening elsewhere in Germany. In Isabel's view, the location of the Wartburg Hotel was too close to the heart of the city for her to enjoy a comfortable night's sleep:

We hadn't many illusions about the favourableness of our situation in case of raids. A short block from the Anhalter Bahnhof, one of Berlin's largest railway stations and around the corner from the Wilhelmstrasse – with its Air Ministry and other buildings attractive to the RAF – we were suitably placed as a target for our own bombs. I guess the Berlin anti-aircraft experts thought so too, as the noise from the big guns on top of the buildings all around us was about as nerve-churning as the falling of the bombs themselves. People say they get hardened to air raids over time. But I defy anyone to hear the wail of the siren and remain unmoved. It was by no means easy on the stomach. The best thing to do, no doubt, is to sleep through raids – if you can. Certainly we couldn't. We would be dressed in five seconds flat, and down the stairs to the ground floor in a few more, collecting our other pale-faced pals en route. 'Grandfather', our ancient Bismarck-moustachioed night porter, would be just ascending in the creaking elevator as we came scurrying down the stairs. It was his duty to alert all guests of the hotel when an alarm sounded. Never, never did he have to knock on our door!

There was a choice of two air-raid shelters in 'the Wart' – the cold cellar and the warm cellar. The first time there was an air raid, we were shown to the cold cellar – through the hotel kitchen, out through an open courtyard where we got the full benefit of the siren's moan and into a sort of store-room. It was a horrid experience sitting there miserably on hard benches in the glare of a strong light, sheltering from our own bombs for two and a half hours; the Enemy to those around us.

But after that, things began to look up. 'Grandfather' proved charitable and told us about the warm cellar, which was much better and even had an old sofa and several easy chairs. Being the first to arrive, we naturally helped ourselves, whereas the

German guests, who were somewhat slower, either stood about or sat on the harder benches. They knew who we were, because we had heard Erne discussing us with some of them. Strange though it may sound, they didn't really seem to mind that we were there and even gossiped freely, thinking, no doubt, that we wouldn't understand. But we did – at least enough to pick up several exciting bits of news. The Germans had been turned back forty miles from Moscow. One girl's brother, who wore glasses, had dropped them and was running so fast in the wrong direction that he hadn't had time to retrieve them. This piece of good news about the German retreat – at a time when Hitler was promising the fall of Moscow in a matter of hours – had come by private air mail, in a letter brought by a pilot returning from the front.

After these sessions, when the blessed 'All Clear' would sound, we would clatter up to Room 7 – our party room – and Doreen would stir up a drink of Klim and Ovaltine from our Red Cross parcels to soothe our nerves. That was another advantage we had over the Germans. I used to wonder what sort of sedative they could find. Some of them even said they would welcome continuous air raids, because if they came, there might be a special coffee ration. It's a fine point: whether the nerves of the Berlin populace would have been more frayed by constant-raids-with-coffee, or by fewer-raids-without-coffee.

And even though Berlin was not the favoured target that winter, her people lived in constant dread of when she would be. The raids of the previous summer had distinctly unnerved them and made them irritable, but Berlin had not yet felt the serious impact of Allied bombing. Then, in the early spring, came heavy attacks on Rostock and Lübeck. In Berlin people heard about them and grew resentful and, not unexpectedly, increasingly fearful. In fact, it was rumoured that all the bombed-out householders of Lübeck and Rostock were advancing on Berlin to swell the ranks of a city that was already seriously overpopulated.

While attending a movie not long after the raids, Isabel and her friends watched the newsreel footage showing the devastation of Lübeck, which prompted a collective hiss to begin rippling through the audience. The effect of this on the Canadian 'outsiders' was to induce them to shrink further down in their seats as they experienced the distinct sensation of guilt by association. In her account of this, Isabel registers the effects of these raids on the population:

> In May, Essen and Cologne became the targets and Berlin whispered the news from street to street the following morning: '1326 planes over Cologne!' That was something to which the reaction was neither irritation nor condemnation, but just the plain stark paralysis of fear. That figure of 1326 planes didn't appear in Berlin newspapers, nor did it come over the German airwaves. Yet it was known all over Berlin – as were many other news items never given out by the press nor heard on the radio.
>
> The answer is simple enough: foreign broadcasts. It was a criminal offence for anyone to be caught listening to the BBC or, for that matter, to any foreign broadcast. But everyone did. I even witnessed it personally once or twice and it was an altogether nerve-wracking performance, with the ear-phones and the radio turned down to the merest whisper. The threat of arrest and possible execution was not an idle one…It was an encouraging insight to find that people still wanted the truth – even at the possible expense of their lives.[37]

The promise of spring

As time went on, some of the *Damenstift* group had broken off from the main body and scattered themselves in various other parts of Berlin. Miss Wilhjelm, with her strong feeling that her charges should preserve their sense of community and solidarity, suggested a Monday afternoon Bible study at her Hospiz St Michael, where the headquarters of the World YMCA was located. In this way, everyone could congregate with a common purpose – to offer up their prayers, study the New Testament and share – in passing – the previous week's developments with one another.

One of the *Damenstift* participants at these weekly gatherings was another Canadian, Catherine Scherfe – formerly an employee of the US embassy in Frankfurt. An innocent victim of reprisals taken due to the detention of German journalists and diplomats in the United States, she had been arrested by the Gestapo the previous summer and dispatched – in error – to the infamous Ravensbrück concentration camp for women. Here she underwent four straight days of questioning by the SS and was a first-hand witness to horrors that left her visibly shaken. Six weeks later, some nameless official decided that she should be transferred from Ravensbrück to join her fellow-Canadians as an internee at Liebenau. Then in mid-September she had become part of the group of 14 released by Herr Inspektor Thomma to take up residence in Berlin while awaiting repatriation.[38]

But, as Isabel notes, even here among her compatriots, Catherine never felt completely at ease.

> There was always the thought in the back of her mind that she was different from the rest of us – a sort of marked woman, whom Gestapo authorities might silently steal away at any moment because she knew too much…So all through that long winter of waiting, she went to her church – not as most of us did, on occasional Sundays – but many days of the week, to attend early Mass on bitterly cold mornings. This was where she found her own private solace and salvation and from which she brought us surprising evidence of the independence of certain members of the Catholic clergy. One morning she came back with the news that the resident priest had made a public avowal of his Bishop's protest against a new State ruling that priests could no longer administer the last Sacrament in the hospitals.[39]

When it came to dealing with the German authorities, the experience Catherine had garnered working for the American consulate in Frankfurt stood her in very good stead. Through her previous employment, she had become familiar with the machinations of German officialdom, and when requested to act as a go-between on behalf of her fellow-Canadians, these unique attributes proved invaluable.

Her fluent German also provided her with a greater insight into the mindset of the people when it came to prevailing attitudes towards the Third Reich. She later reported to Canadian authorities that during her stay in Berlin she had noticed undercurrents of discontent regarding the Nazi regime and outspoken disgust among the majority of the Germans she came in contact with over the treatment of the Jews. On the other hand, she was firm in her conviction that none of this would prevent the German people as a whole from hanging on for as long as they could. Although it had a dramatic effect on his listeners, she was of the opinion that even Hitler's landmark speech in the spring of 1942 – in which he as much as admitted that the war on the Eastern Front had been a disaster – failed to induce a widespread sense of futility. The Führer had declared that the war would last one more winter – a statement which stunned the populace, but in Catherine's view it was still not enough to affect the national will to carry on.[40]

Isabel's reaction was much the same, although her compassion for the plight of the German people is perhaps more vividly expressed:

When Hitler – in his speech of April 25th – actually admitted mistakes in the previous winter's campaign, promised that such errors would be rectified in plans for the winter to come, assured bereaved mothers that death by freezing was not painful, and told his people they must be prepared to sacrifice more and more – then, it seemed to me, his people realised, perhaps for the first time, that their Führer was human after all, could make mistakes. And they were afraid. I saw the Brown Shirts on Parade, after the speech that same day. They had been harangued at the usual great length. But I thought that the result was not the same as usual. Instead of the faces I had seen so often before – empty faces, wiped clean of any expression whatsoever – these faces looked troubled and downcast.[41]

Another Canadian, Gwendolyne Foreshaw, also among the group of 14 transferred from Liebenau to Berlin, had fared even less well than Catherine. After being arrested by the Gestapo in Amsterdam when the Nazis occupied the city, she had been shipped off to a nearby internment camp and treated with relative indulgence by the Dutch guards. However, five weeks later she was relegated to the ravages of Ravensbrück until her transfer to Liebenau came though. This occurred only a few short weeks before Thomma's decision to allow the Canadians to proceed to Berlin to await further developments on the diplomatic front.[42]

From time to time, small glimmers of hope had surfaced as the result of an exchange of inter-governmental memos concerning their repatriation, but these generally proved unproductive in the long run. Setting the wheels of bureaucracy into motion was a notoriously slow process, and one which could well be applied across the board to all diplomatic dealings and negotiations between the governments involved. Nothing was ever as straightforward as it seemed at first glance, but the thought of abandoning their campaign for repatriation never seems to have occurred to any of these intrepid women. Sooner or later, the power of Providence would prevail.

Among the Canadian women, the solitary and philosophical Olga was most probably best equipped to withstand the many disappointments and setbacks that had followed them to Berlin. Olga's unshakeable faith is echoed in her musings on the nature of hope and the part it had played in their lives:

> Since that morning when the first shells had struck the *Zamzam*, we had hoped – for a neutral South American port, for a mid-ocean transfer, for assistance from the American consul, for release from Liebenau, for exit permits from Berlin, for passage back to Africa. We had hoped and one by one, we had seen most

of our hopes defeated. Only Hope itself lived on to transcend all our smaller hopes...[43]

There were still lessons to be learned in Berlin. Out of its hopelessness, we learned hope and a renewed dependence on both God and Man...The very atmosphere of Berlin – the shortage of food, the suffering of the Jews, the discouragement felt as the casualty lists swelled, even the wild cheering in the streets – all indicated that, even in Berlin, no man was sufficient unto himself...One thing the depressive air which hung over Berlin had taught us was that – in reality – we were all one. It had taught us to draw apart from ourselves and – at a distance – view our relationship with the world rather than the world in relationship to ourselves...It was all one and the same and there was hope for all.[44]

During the bleak mid-winter of 1942, the impact of these laudable sentiments may well have been lost on the citizens of Berlin, although the Canadians – as a group – still held on tenaciously to the illusive prospect of freedom. Although the outlook for the future remained uncertain at best, they firmly maintained their resolve to take life one day at a time and make the best of whatever came their way. Isabel wrote,

> Strange, how so often I could feel much sorrier for the Germans we saw about us than for ourselves...It was a sad city, that city of Berlin, and grew progressively sadder. So very many hopeless-looking people. We, ourselves, did a lot of laughing, in one way and another, and whenever we did it in public, in street-cars, the underground or cafés, faces would look up all around us – bewildered faces. What could there possibly be to laugh about?[45]

Each Tuesday afternoon the *Damenstift* became a beehive of industry as they met in one another's rooms to sew and embroider under the expert tutelage of Fräulein Keller, a veteran German missionary who had served in India for 27 years. 'Auntie Keller', as Isabel refers to her, was almost desperately willing to pass on the finely honed skills she had acquired over the years, as it also offered her the opportunity to mingle with her new-found Canadian friends and to speak her mind openly without fear of being reported for seditious commentary. When at home, she had to remain constantly on guard, as the doctor who was owner of the apartment building where she and her immediate family lived was known as 'a good Party man'.

The long winter days came and went; however, the arrival of the month of March brought both Vida Steele and Allison 'Jamie' Henderson something heartening and unexpected, which provided a well-timed bright spot in the dreary winter days. Ten months had passed since they and their husbands had said their last brief good-byes in north Germany before the men of the *Zamzam* had been marched off to the merchant marine prison camp. In her family memoirs, Vida recalls her joy and excitement at the news:

> The Red Cross supplied forms for us so we could write to our husbands and also back to Canada. Thus I could keep in contact with my children. On March 1st, with special permission from government officials, we wives were allowed to visit our husbands in a prisoner-of-war camp on the Polish border. We met for an hour and each word we spoke had to be heard and understood by the German official who sat with us ... Then in May, believing we might be free to return home, we applied for another permit to see our husbands. This was granted and we un-registered with the police in Berlin. After a certain amount of travelling time, we had to register with the police in Tost. This is how they kept track of us. My husband was not well and it was hard to say good-bye knowing that he was suffering.[46]

For Isabel and Kitsi, the two socialites of the group, life in Berlin continued to be full of surprises. Once the Americans had been unceremoniously removed for internment at Bad Nauheim, they were left to their own devices, but gradually they began making new acquaintances. Among those in Isabel's new and ever-expanding circle was the last remaining Irish Free State diplomat in Berlin. Having learned of the Canadians' plight, he gallantly issued Isabel and Kitsi an invitation to the St Patrick's Day party he was throwing at the Irish embassy on 17 March. According to Isabel's account of the festivities, no expense was spared in the interests of assuring that the guests of Eire would enjoy and remember this celebratory occasion.

St Patrick's Day in Berlin – the idea seemed somehow incongruous. The Professor, who knew I was attending the Irish 'At Home', sent me a newspaper clipping – the *Berliner Zeitung's* description of the affair. Under the heading 'Aus der Diplomatie', the news reporter stated that 'Close to three hundred guests from the Diplomatic Corps as well as Representatives of the State, Party and the Military were among those invited by the Irish Diplomat. From the Foreign Office the presence of Undersecretary Woermann was noted and the Press Department of the Reich's Administration was represented by Dr Brauweiler.'[47]

On arrival, Isabel and Kitsi were directed upstairs to an improvised cloakroom, and Isabel found it impossible to refrain from commenting on her impressions of the 'Ladies' facilities. When they had occasion to visit these during the course of the evening's festivities, it became immediately obvious that their host's generosity had not extended as far as it might have. There was no soap and no toilet paper. Berlin was conspicuously bare of such commodities in those days – but they both registered surprise that the Irish diplomat had not tapped into his private supply of these necessities of life, although – in the dining-room – real coffee flowed and stimulated the *ersatzed* German palates to the point of near intoxication.

As we came downstairs again we found ourselves in a line, waiting to sign the Guest Book. Directly in front of us were three little men from the Japanese Diplomatic Corps. It was a strange feeling to sign my name after theirs – and I added a great flourish to my home address: Vancouver, CANADA. Then we wandered in the direction everybody else was taking, after being received by our host, and soon found the centre of attraction, which was the dining-room. It was a long, gracious room, but there was nothing gracious about the crowd pushing and jostling one another to get near the table. The poor starved Germans – the nation's finest, the élite, the cream of society, the diplomats of all Europe, and a German General resplendent in grey and scarlet – were so deeply affected by the sight of FOOD that it was almost impossible to watch them. Never have I seen cakes and ice cream disappear faster at a children's party.

Kitsi and I wouldn't have stood a chance in that stampede had we not been spotted by Frau Fuchs – an acquaintance met only once before – but once met, never to be forgotten. Fortunately, neither had she forgotten us. She bore down on us, a ship in full sail, her prow loaded with jewels on the bosom and a garden of flowers on her head. Such a hat could not have bloomed outside of Germany. That was one helpful aspect of life in Berlin for us who would occasionally venture into higher society with only shipwrecked wardrobes. Style was non-existent. It was a case of 'Anything goes'. So, Frau Fuchs, wife of a German High Commissioner, appeared in her flower garden, and Kitsi sported a simple outfit of mine which had been new four years before. To my perhaps prejudiced eye, Kitsi looked far smarter…

I engaged Frau Fuchs in what I hoped would be some enlightening gossip. I was certain that she would know her 'Who's Who' intimately, so when I asked her who was who, she replied, lowering her naturally penetrating voice to a confidential whisper 'My dear, don't you know that it is the riff-raff of the country who are in the prominent positions today… with a few exceptions, of course?' No doubt she was referring to her highly placed husband. Well, I, too, had heard that this was the case, but it was interesting to have it confirmed there, in the upper crust of the Nazi social pie.[48]

The *Damenstift* diplomats

With the welcome arrival of spring-like weather, the spirits of the *Damenstift* occupants at the dreary old 'Wart' lifted accordingly. The cold, cloudy winter mists that hung over the city had begun to lift, and flower vendors mingled in the streets with the women, the wounded, the foreign labourers and children at play. All winter long, one after the other, the Canadians had pestered the authorities – from embassies, to the Foreign Office and even to the Gestapo. Isabel claims to have drafted so many petitions stating their case that even she had begun to find the time-worn phrases almost meaningless.

As they sat up in bed early one morning, in a moment of sheer frivolity she and Kitsi had even composed a letter to the Führer appealing to his 'well-known magnanimity'; however, he never seemed to stay in Berlin long enough for them to learn of his arrival and deliver the letter by hand. In the year 1942, it is on record that Hitler only spent a grand total of 25 days in the Reich's capital,[49] so – had there been even the remotest possibility of carrying out their naïve scheme – the opportunities for them to deliver their letter would have been very limited indeed. The old saying about the road to Hell being paved with good intentions would certainly have applied to this particular plan. Hell would freeze over before to their plea for special consideration would get past the nearest wastepaper basket. Yet still they soldiered bravely on against all odds. Nothing ventured, nothing gained:

> It was a protracted siege. After the American Embassy was closed, we took on the Swiss – with occasional side forays to the Swedish and Turkish legations which we thought might provide a circumnavigating exit. There was even one exciting week when we took it upon our indomitable selves to storm the Gestapo. Somebody at the Swiss Embassy had said: 'Well, try it if you want to. Perhaps you'll be satisfied then that if we can't do it for you, certainly you won't succeed in getting yourselves out of this country on your own. Still, one never can tell. I believe some British women did get out, soon after the War started, by going to No. 8, Hermann Goering Strasse.'
>
> So, armed with this secret and exciting address, off we went. And – to our utter confusion – were welcomed with a smile by an armed sentry inside its doors. When we stated our business, he

took us up some prison-like stairs to a man who, he explained, would be the right man for us because he spoke English.[50] He did speak English, although very little, and to make matters worse he had a harelip, so it was difficult to understand him in any language. However, he was most polite and responded with, 'But of course, why shouldn't you be allowed to leave Germany?' and sent us off to the Foreign Police, who promptly sent us back again. This time a different and less minor Gestapo official received us and told us, less politely and much more firmly, that our exit permit would come from the Foreign Office, through the appropriate Embassy – implying by tone if not in actual words, that we should get the hell out of there and not bother him any further…So there we were…right back where we had started.

Truly, our experience with the mañana principle was never more valuable than when put to use in helping us sustain our diplomatic forays in Berlin. The Swiss Embassy people were less defeatist than the Americans had been, and never frankly discouraged us. They would tell us – always – that they were working on our case and hoped that something would be arranged in time. The German Foreign Office said the same, monotonously and redundantly.

The major difficulty seemed to be the means of transporting us home, presuming the diplomatic details of exchange could be completed. And of course, we horribly persistent *Zamzamers* soon found the answer to that. Why not send us home with the returning American diplomats?[51]

In reality, there was plenty of time to make such an arrangement, since the Americans seemed likely to languish a few months longer at Bad Nauheim. Not only that, but the *Zamzam* delegation – with Isabel at the helm – had actually persuaded someone at the Swiss legation to send a cable to the Canadian government to propose this possibility. For reasons never adequately explained, the Canadian government failed to respond. Possibly the overworked bureaucrats involved in such negotiations did not welcome any unsolicited suggestions concerning the matter – even when they came from those directly affected. There was also the remote possibility that diplomatic overtures had already been made and the officials involved were busy laying the groundwork for just such an operation. In any event, both the Swiss and the German Foreign Office provided the delighted Canadians with a small ray of hope by telling them that they considered this possibility an entirely reasonable solution to their ongoing dilemma.[52]

At this point, the stranded Canadians were unaware of the existence of an official communiqué from the German Foreign Office dated 19 December that was forwarded to its counterpart in Canada recognising the presence in Berlin of nine Canadian women formerly held in a German internment camp and specifically mentioning those who had been taken prisoner following the sinking of the *Zamzam*. The missive – marked 'urgent' – went on to say that since no German women had been interned in Canada, the possibility was being explored of including these Canadian women in the repatriation arrangements being negotiated for the return of the recently interned American diplomats and journalists.[53]

A specific repatriation date for the Americans had yet to be finalised; however, it had been agreed in principle that they would return to North America via the neutral port of Lisbon. Given that the US government was agreeable to the safe return of all German civilians currently being interned in America, in exchange for the Americans interned in Germany, it would only be a matter of time and patience before the details of a reciprocal repatriation were worked out to the satisfaction of all concerned.[54] Nor did it do any harm that, by incredible coincidence, Norman Robertson, Canada's Secretary of State for Foreign Affairs, happened to be an old family friend of Isabel Guernsey's parents in Vancouver. Behind the scenes, Robertson had been attempting to move heaven and earth to help effect the release of the Canadians in Berlin, and on 3 February 1942 he fired off an urgent telegram to the Swiss consul general in Berlin:

> British Minister, Berne, informs us German authorities prepared to permit repatriation nine Canadian women from Berlin with the United States diplomatic corps on understanding Canadian authorities will permit repatriation to Germany of an equal number of German women including those interned at Kingston. STOP. British minister is being requested by cable today to agree to suggested arrangement on behalf of Canadian government. STOP. Please inform me what arrangements are proposed by yourself as representative Protecting Power Germany with regard to repatriation of German women in Canada. Understand German authorities wish them to accompany German official party from the United States. STOP.

Norman Robertson's message left no room for doubt. Canada was prepared to undertake a reciprocal exchange arrangement as soon as it could be arranged. Many months later, he would receive a profuse letter of personal thanks from Isabel for his efforts on behalf of herself and her compatriots. She also extended apologies 'for being such a damn nuisance for the past year', and closed with the words 'What a business it has been!'[55]

But before any of this came to light, the Canadian women in Berlin were facing what seemed to be an eternally long spell of sitting on their hands while waiting to discover exactly when the interned American journalists and diplomats would be released to make the return journey back to the States. But more importantly, if they left without the Zamzamers, the general consensus was that their last chance for repatriation would have slipped beyond their grasp. They would simply have to resign themselves to the grim thought of spending the remainder of the war in Berlin. Not a very encouraging prospect at the best of times!

With this in mind, in mid-April a few of the more disgruntled Canadians, including Olga, had taken it upon themselves to visit the Foreign Office in Berlin and request permission for permits to return to Liebenau. The very place from which they so eagerly awaited release had suddenly acquired an unforeseen allure, with its bracing country air and peaceful surroundings. The increasing scarcity of food in Berlin was also a factor in this decision, as well as the housing situation, which was becoming increasingly difficult.

To compound the situation, the rooms on the top floor of the Wartburg Hotel had been requisitioned by the SS, which meant that the last remaining *Damenstift* occupants – Kitsi and Isabel, Doreen and Jamie – would be forced to find other accommodation on extremely short notice. New laws had been issued prohibiting residence in a hotel for longer than two weeks, and these were scheduled to be put into effect in the near future. Perhaps Liebenau, after all, would prove to be their final refuge.

To their great surprise, the request to return to Liebenau was denied on the grounds that they were due to receive exit permits and a passage back to America in a few weeks' time. This news served to rekindle their hopes, but only to a certain degree. The pessimists among them remained doubtful. They had received similar promises before, and learned from bitter experience that the assurances they had been given were little more than hollow promises made with the intention of keeping the persistent Canadians at bay. For one thing, the officials at the German Foreign Office had matters of far greater urgency to deal with, and furthermore, experience had taught them that if they were quick to assure the supplicants that good news would soon be forthcoming, they would be rewarded by a brief respite from another onslaught of polite but persistent Canadian-style harassment. By now, even Isabel had grown dubious of any promises, but had still not entirely abandoned hope that, by some miracle, word of their release would eventually come through.

And, as if to herald the arrival of spring, this time there was actually some truth to the rumours emanating from the Foreign Office's inner sanctum. Isabel records the ensuing ecstasy this news created in the *Damenstift*:

Then one day, suddenly, in April there was word at the Foreign Office that we might expect to sail for home within a few weeks with the American diplomats on the first crossing of the Swedish-based exchange ship the *Drottningholm*. The *Damenstift* turned almost turtle with excitement. I myself was a little sceptical when I found that the Swiss Embassy knew nothing about this arrangement, or said they didn't. But Doreen and Jamie, who had talked to Dr Bauer, the polite young man with whom we dealt at the Foreign Office, were sure he really meant it this time. They started to pack that very night.[56]

Not that there was much packing to be done. Many members of the *Damenstift* – particularly the missionaries – had lost most of their belongings in the *Zamzam* disaster, and those who had salvaged anything had divided their clothes among the other passengers. During the cold nights on the *Dresden*, they had tried to distribute clothing so that everyone could be kept reasonably warm. And since their arrival in Berlin six months earlier, no cards for clothing rations had been issued to them. In fact, the few clothes they possessed between them had been made from cotton fabric sent by the Red Cross or had been passed on to them, second-hand, while they were interned at Liebenau.

And then, just as suddenly as it surfaced, on 4 May the whole repatriation scheme fell apart. No Canadians would be allowed aboard the *Drottningholm*, since it was scheduled to transport only the Americans being held in Munich and Bad Nauheim. Unlike the Canadians, who had established their own policy for the exchange of prisoners based on the principle of prisoner for prisoner, the exchange of American prisoners was not being made person for person. All Americans who wanted to leave the Third Reich were to be guaranteed a passage home, with the United States reciprocating. Olga describes the situation from her perspective:

> This policy meant that if a certain number of Canadian women were to be sent from Germany, an equal number of German

women must be released from Canada. As the boat docked only in New York harbour, this involved the passage of the Germans from Canada through the United States. Existing technicalities had prevented adequate arrangements. In retaliation, the German government refused to issue our exit permits. We were to remain in Berlin.

We heard of Swiss and Canadian attempts to make arrangements for passage on another neutral ship, provided neutral passage back for the Germans could be guaranteed. But no direct word ever reached us. Then on May 23rd, we received news that the *Drottningholm* had left Lisbon harbour the day before. The first load of exchange prisoners had sailed.[57]

In the scheme of things, ironing out these details on paper should have been a relatively uncomplicated matter; yet the amount of time it took to negotiate a mutually satisfactory solution was enough to delay the process of repatriation and prevent the Canadians from inclusion as passengers on the 'freedom train' to Lisbon in mid-May. They would simply have to remain on the waiting list for the next train – if, indeed, arrangements for a second freedom train were successfully orchestrated. And the question of precisely when this would take place – if ever – had yet to be addressed.

The garden house

By mid-May, the mood of the Canadians was brightened by having solved the disquieting problem of finding new accommodation on relatively short notice. The new hotel regulations had created a potentially impossible situation, and it was with a sigh of relief that seven of them – including Olga – were able to move to Konradshöhe on the outskirts of Berlin.

It was a five-room summer house fully furnished and equipped with dishes and bedding – the most lavish quarters we had lived in since leaving America…There were no electric lights and

165

since we were within the Berlin blackout area, it was dangerous to burn candles. As soon as it became dark, we went to bed. The neighbouring cottage had a built-in air-raid shelter which we would be permitted to use in case of attack. The gardens and fruit trees on the property would yield many of the fresh fruits and vegetables our ration cards had deprived us of throughout the winter months. Twice a week we were given permission to gather fallen branches for firewood in the nearby forests, but no one was allowed to break branches from the trees or destroy standing timber. As a result all the underbrush had been cleared away, leaving the forest floor immaculately clean.[58]

Kitsi and Isabel had also found a solution to their housing dilemma, and moved into what Isabel referred to as their 'beautiful greenhouse', where – if the worst came to the worst – they were at least guaranteed a spot in the sun for the summer. Isabel's and Kitsi's 'Greenhouse' was a small furnished cottage situated close to the Wannsee which had been offered to them for the season at the behest of Isabel's much-loved Professor. In fact, only a matter of months had passed since Isabel and Doreen had spent that memorable Christmas Eve with him in his beautiful home on the Wannsee. Although it had been left largely unspoken, both Isabel and the Professor were both aware that – as a Jew in Hitler's Berlin – the Professor was living on borrowed time. But in the weeks or months he had left, he was determined that, come what may, he was going to help his young Canadian friends find a suitable alternative to their room on the third floor of the hotel on Anhalterstrasse. Ironically, just months before, in January 1942, the now infamous Wannsee Conference, formalising Adolf Hitler's 'final solution' plans for the remaining Jews in Europe, had taken place only a short distance from the country cottage where Isabel and Kitsi were revelling in their new-found paradise.

Initially, the Professor's elderly cousin who owned the cottage had been aghast at the idea of anyone even attempting to inhabit the Greenhouse. It was far too primitive. The stove was unreliable. The plumbing didn't work, the roof leaked, and the mosquitoes were due to arrive at any moment. But when the Professor assured her that these women were hardy Canadians and quite accustomed to 'roughing it in the bush', she was finally persuaded, and Isabel was ecstatic.

I remember the day he first took us to view the Greenhouse property…We went to her former neighbours to collect the keys of the Greenhouse from their gardener, who had once also been the Greenhouse gardener. He treated the Professor with deference and a sort of respectful pity. His employers, still people of Aryan importance in Berlin, would acknowledge the Professor's bow if he passed them on the street – but nothing more.

What a strange and ridiculous situation a World War can create. I, a Canadian stranded in Nazi Germany, was among the rare few who could dare to be friendly to a Jew and could live on Jewish property without official criticism. In fact, before we finally moved to the Greenhouse I had visited the German Foreign Office to obtain their sanction. They had nothing against it – if the Jewish owner could get the permission to lease.

Trying to get that permission was fun – at least for us – though not perhaps for our Jewish lawyer, who did his best to help. When we moved in to the Greenhouse, I had in my possession a contract, drawn up in proper German legal terminology – but it had not yet been signed by the necessary authority, the Bürgermeister of Zehlendorf. Since we couldn't wait for him to sign it, encouraged by the naughty Professor, we moved in anyway, thereby adding yet another furrow to the brow of the already overtaxed lawyer. It had all been the Professor's fault, really. Nothing was going to stand in the way of our moving to the Greenhouse. From that first day, when we saw the property and responded to its possibilities, nothing would stop him, short of being taken away himself. Mamzel, his housekeeper, was anxious. She felt he was making himself too conspicuous, trotting back and forth from his garden to ours, the great yellow Star on his left breast a blazing advertisement to everyone of what he was. There was little danger in our fraternising with a Jew (that, indeed, was to be expected of the British!). For the Jew, however, it was not so healthy. But the joys of our garden, the Professor's last Paradise on earth, were enough to more than counterbalance – in his mind – any danger he might be running. And besides, I suspect he really quite enjoyed the drama of living a little more dangerously.[59]

Now happily ensconced in the Greenhouse, the professor's charges – aided and abetted by their gracious benefactor – had immediately set about making their new quarters into a charming little country hideaway. Days were spent carting away old flowerpots and installing the bamboo batiks and Egyptian wall hangings which the Professor had taken out of storage for them, as well as a Tyrolean cowbell, an old mismatched set of china and an ancient dispatch case which served as their letterbox.

With the onset of the first warm days, the fruit trees in the garden had come into blossom one after another. First the cherry, then the plum and peach trees, and finally the luxuriant white lilac wafted its scent in all directions. For the two Canadian tenants, life in the Greenhouse seemed like a small-scale Shangri-La. In the evenings and on rainy days, Kitsi would sit and read, while Isabel worked on the manuscript she had already begun writing several months earlier – the story of the voyage of seven Canadian strangers who had set sail for Cape Town and reached war-torn Germany instead.

The unwritten fate of the Professor was never far from their thoughts. Nor were their fears unjustified. Only a month earlier, the lower floor of his house had been arbitrarily taken over for the use of the Wehrmacht. They also learned, to their horror, that one day early in March he had been informed that he should be ready to leave for the limbo of Poland in twenty-four hours or less. Through the intervention of an influential friend, at the eleventh hour the deportation order had been rescinded and he had been told that his reprieve might last for another six months if his luck held out. The remaining days and hours of his life were slowly but inexorably trickling away like the grains of sand in an hourglass, yet his inner despair was carefully disguised – and perhaps even sublimated – by the sheer enjoyment he received from brightening the lives of his two Canadian friends in their sun-drenched Greenhouse.

Isabel and Kitsi enjoyed the thought of living dangerously almost as much as their self-appointed guardian. It was great fun to wake up in the Greenhouse in the morning, not knowing what excitement the new day might bring. There was, for instance, a heart-stopping Sunday morning, just before they had properly moved in, but were already working in the garden. Both were busily weeding their strawberry patch and enjoying the Wannsee air as a cuckoo called to them at regular five-minute intervals. Life was, indeed, beautiful, when into this idyllic scene two uniformed figures strode, and after a cursory 'Heil Hitler' demanded that the ladies produce their passports.

It may have been a Sunday, but it wasn't an unreasonable or unexpected request. No German even crossed the street without his papers of identification, so we put down our tools and fetched our passports for inspection. It didn't take long. One of the men read out the details, although he encountered some difficulties with the pronunciation of our names, but we stood in stony dignified silence and didn't help him out, while the other wrote down the details in his little book. Then they asked us a rhetorical question. You might even call it negative affirmation. 'You're not Jews?' whereupon the two soldiers disappeared down the garden path, never to be seen again.

The Professor then re-appeared from behind the raspberry canes where he had hurriedly concealed his presence when he saw them approaching. 'What did they want?' He was excited and nervous but once he heard the answer, he was both relieved and amused. Just a routine check-up on newcomers, he decided…

There was another afternoon later on, when Kitsi came rushing in to tell me a soldier was coming up our garden path. My German was more adequate than hers and it generally fell to me to deal with any strangers. Steeling myself to this new encounter, I went out. There stood a tired-looking young soldier of the Third Reich. He wanted to know if he could have our grass, growing long and luxuriant under the apple trees, for his rabbits. As it turned out, he couldn't have it, as it had already been promised to someone else – the Professor's housekeeper.[60]

They also discovered that the Professor had an old friend in the Wannsee area – someone who probably should no longer have considered himself a friend. Being a prominent Berlin doctor and ostensibly a good Party man, what business could he possibly have that would involve consorting with a Jew? Sufficient, it seemed for the Professor, to arrange through him for Kitsi and Isabel to pick up their midday meal from the Segelhaus at the Wannsee Yacht Club, where the Professor's doctor friend was an important member. The true extent of his importance was only impressed upon them the first time they sallied forth to fetch their midday Eintopf (casserole) – that most popular of dishes in wartime Berlin.

After a while, a pompous fat little man disengaged himself from the flurry of waiters and asked us, rather peremptorily, what we were doing there. We asked, politely, for our Eintopf. He asked – less politely – who had sent us; to which we answered, haughtily, 'Herr Doktor Richter.'[61]

The name had a magical ring, and to it the small fat man responded with bows and smiles and a knowing nod. 'Ach so! The ladies the Herr Doktor told me of. His friends! I am at your service, meine Damen. What can I do for you?' When they again mentioned the Eintopf, he looked surprised. 'But surely, something more is desired? I have many things on my menu for any friend of the Herr Doktor. Whatever I have is yours.'

When Isabel stubbornly stuck to the Eintopf, and said that it would be their regular daily requirement, he appeared quite crestfallen. How could the poor fellow possibly know that the small matter of finance entered into the picture? Frills, such as Herr Dr Richter's friends would normally order, would have been very costly, so when it came to the moment of paying for the simple Eintopf, he was once again surprised. But surely, they did not intend to pay for it?...Yes, this was, indeed, their intention. And in the end he accepted this rather unusual situation, saying that for the Herr Doktor's friends, it would be a nominal sum. They only discovered the next day – after watching him hastily slip their precious money into his pocket – that he had charged them double the regular price for an Eintopf.

Regardless of the mediocre fare and the exorbitant price, to the two 'country girls' the frequent midday visits to the good Doktor's elegant Yacht Club made for a pleasant break in their daily routine. All morning they would weed and dig and plant in their garden, before heading off to fetch their Eintopf. Without having to worry about using the cottage's temperamental stove, they could simply take a tray out to a spot in the garden, where white garden chairs and a table sank into long green grass, and the perfume of white lilacs wafted over them.[62]

Although living at opposite ends of the outer reaches of Berlin, the two small bands of marooned Canadian women made a point of keeping in touch with each other in the midst of the increasingly tedious waiting game. Often members of the group of seven who were living in the large summer house in Konradshöhe would make the long trip over to Kitsi and Isabel's Wannsee Greenhouse and marvel at the cosy atmosphere the two friends had created from next to nothing.

Isabel notes that, while they may have been removed from the hustle and bustle of the inner city, their simple country cottage was clearly a popular destination:

> There were others, too, who found it a pleasant place. Our friends came first out of curiosity – but those who came to scoff, remained

to envy, and came again. Rare was the day that no visitor was heard pulling our Professor-made bell – the cowbell from the Tyrol, which hung in an apple tree with a length of Red Cross string stretching from it to hang over our garden gate and be pulled from the outside…

Our entertaining was done al fresco and we issued no special invitations, but our visitors still came. One Saturday morning we counted up, with some dismay, fourteen people who had asked if they might come that afternoon, which would mean a quite heroic effort. However, Heaven took pity on us, rolled up its clouds in the late morning, opened their sluice-gates by noon, and flooded the countryside. In another hour, everything under our leaking living-room roof was damp, but dampened, too, were the spirits of our prospective guests. Only two, of the expected multitude came to tea in the puddles.[63]

Some of their male guests also rendered invaluable service in exchange for the warm hospitality they always received. Neither Isabel nor Kitsi ever asked them directly, but if they arrived on the scene and found their hostesses working in the garden, it seemed only natural to offer them assistance.

Perhaps the most enthusiastic of their so-called Men's Auxiliary was Herr Doktor Thun, Isabel's Czechoslovakian-born 'guardian angel' from the Swiss embassy, who often brought with him the latest confidential embassy news. He would roll up, unheralded, on his bicycle and pass on the rumour of the day: that they were slated to accompany the second American exchange transport. Then on his next visit, he would tell them that their names had been erased again. On a beautiful Sunday in early June, he came by with a friend to take Isabel and Kitsi out on the Wannsee for a tour in his boat. They must, he insisted, have one day of rest and relaxation, and so off they went, the four of them, in two boats – Thun's racing rowing boat, and the little paddleboat which the Professor had thoughtfully reconditioned for their special use. It was a fine hot day in June, and the waters of the Wannsee were crowded with every description of craft which could be propelled without fuel. It seemed as if all of Berlin migrated to the Wannsee on warm summer Sundays to absorb from the sun's impartial rays the vitamins they couldn't get from wartime food.

Starting off in fine form, the paddlers threaded their way skillfully through the early morning aquatic traffic jam. Even Kitsi and Isabel, inexperienced in the art of navigating German-style paddle-boats, set off with a will. It took less than five minutes before they realised their inadequacies. The men's four-oared racing scull was almost having to back-water to keep pace with their snail-like progress. Undaunted, Thun suggested that each boat should have one experienced paddler on board. A simple transfer would solve the problem and help to balance their respective speed – however their headway was still impeded by the neophytes' lack of experience. By Thun's calculations, they must reach Moorlake – five long miles up the Wannsee – by noon or there would be nothing left for lunch. The hungry masses would have gobbled up everything in sight.

It was at least one o'clock before they arrived at their destination, and Thun was right. The huge and popular restaurant at Moorlake was overflowing with throngs of Berlin's would-be merrymakers. By boat, by foot, by S-Bahn, they had come by the hundreds.

Thun, an old customer of the place, collared a waiter he knew – a pale, haggard specimen, but cheerful. Yes, yes...he would bring us, almost immediately, four beers and four lunches. Then minutes later he came back with a great clatter of superfluous cutlery. Then minutes more and he brought us two beers. Twelve minutes more and he appeared with three mixed vegetable plates. We never did get the other two beers, nor the fourth plate. Our host and his friend did their level best to imagine that this was fun – like all the rest of the pleasure-starved Germans. Kitsi and I did our best too. But our spirits longed for our peaceful Greenhouse.

Then it was into the boats again and on our way for the long paddle home. Here and there, as we struggled along, we saw boats moored in the rushes at the lake's edge, their owners ashore. Such pieces of shoreline could be leased for the season by those wanting a private spot – for picnicking. Not very private, but nevertheless a space to call their own.

It was six o'clock by the time we reached our familiar shores again. We had the Professor coming for dinner, and some Swiss friends dropping in afterwards to drink guest-provided champagne in honour of Kitsi's twenty-eighth birthday. Bruised and aching in every bone, over-burnished by a long day in the sun, I don't know how we summoned courage to attack the wretched stove that evening. But we did, and somehow that creature of unpredictable personality, of whom we despondently expected the worst, co-operated as never before…Dinner was ready, although his hostesses were still in bathing-suits when the Professor arrived at seven. He was quite content to keep one eye on the bubbling pot on the stove, the other admiring our table, while we dressed. The table centre-piece was Kitsi's birthday-cake, made by Mamzel and decorated by me with one candle and the first pink peony from our garden…[64]

And so the incipient joys of spring slipped by, every day bringing some new flower or shrub to blossom in the Greenhouse garden. Rediscovering an established, but long-neglected garden is an exciting prospect. When Kitsi and Isabel first moved in, primroses and forsythia were blooming in a far corner. They had raked up the dead leaves piled by the winds of winter against the garden wall and, to their delight, had found pale green-leaved lilies of the valley. Then came the lovely white lilac. And one morning the Professor arrived with a branch of wild laburnum – its golden blossom lighting up a corner of the pine wood as he came through.

The whole of Wannsee was excitingly lovely, that early summer. Strange that we – the Enemy within – should see it at its best in the midst of a war. Except on Sundays, when the masses came, bringing fumes of gasoline to spoil the air of Wannsee's winding streets dappled by sun and the shadow of age-old trees, the air was perfumed with lilac and jasmine, wisteria and wild roses, and the scent of pine needles, hot on the ground under the June sun. It was lyric and unreal – our Greenhouse life. The Professor had a description for it: everything hovered between dreams and reality.[65]

When the news came, with exactly one week's notice, that they were to leave their Greenhouse – to leave Germany, to return home – it came, momentarily, as something as sorrowful as it was exciting. To Kitsi, now two years married, the glorious weeks spent in the garden Greenhouse represented her first real experience as a householder. To Isabel, it was the responsibility of having helped create a kind of happy mirage for a sad old man. The thought of shattering the illusion was painful.

The news came, ironically, from the Professor himself. Being without benefit of a telephone in the Greenhouse, they were beholden to him or to Mamzel for taking and relaying messages. On a Friday afternoon, Kitsi and Isabel were entertaining at tea in the garden on the white table in the long green grass, with snowballs and currant bushes all around and a façade of raspberry canes.

> Tea was over, and the shadows were lengthening when the Professor appeared – as he often did at that time in the afternoon. He almost always knew our programme in advance and if we had guests coming, he would make a late entry, coming in the back way through the pine wood, carrying his yellow-starred coat over his arm, so that he could appear as if he were one of us and not embarrass our friends nor himself. He would pretend to have simply come by to do the evening watering of the garden. But the pretence would be easily dismissed and he would sit down among us and proceed to cast his spell over one after another of our friends who had not yet met him.[66]

And it was to one of these happy garden tea-parties that the Professor brought the news. Herr Doktor Bauer of the Foreign Office had telephoned that he wished to see Isabel at 11.00 the next morning. The Professor gave the message with a smile, but this time he would not stay to meet their guests. Instead, he wandered off towards the Greenhouse and was suddenly – in Isabel's eyes – transformed into a bowed and broken old man.

Alarming thoughts sprang to my mind. Why this sudden call from the Foreign Office? Heaven knows, we had called upon them often enough in the past nine months, but never before had they so honoured us. Did it mean perhaps the end of our beloved Greenhouse? Had the Bürgermeister of Zehlendorf refused to sign the form and declared that we must leave our preciously precarious existence?

A few minutes later, I found the Professor stretched out on the wicker chaise longue in our Greenhouse living-room – his face an obscure mask…'What's wrong?' I asked him. 'What does Herr Bauer want? Must we leave the Greenhouse?' Yes, my dear, I think so,' he said, gently. 'He wishes to talk to you about your Ausreise.'

My heart skipped a beat. Ausreise, exit permit, Home! But the sad, tired old face came between me and my vision – I couldn't bear it. Oh God, do something – let there be some way out of this for him too. How can we leave him? He loves life – how can we take it from him?

I only heard, many months later, of his death. How or when, perhaps I shall never know. A mutual friend once said to me: 'When you go, it will be the death of that old man.' I hope he was right. I hope Kitsi is right, when she writes to comfort me: 'Don't grieve too much. Think of the darling Greenhouse – and our last happy weeks there. He loved us so much…I think his sad, loving old heart just stopped beating one day – too tired, and lonely. I can picture him, curled up like a child asleep on his couch – smiling in his sleep.' If he died like that, smiling with thoughts of us, then perhaps Life is, after all, a beautiful gift.[67]

6

Repatriation

13–30 June 1942

Patience rewarded

The second and last so-called freedom train was due to board its hand-picked passengers – South and Central America diplomats, returning Americans, and the Canadian Zamzamers tacked on at the last minute – at eleven o'clock on the night of Saturday 13 June. The *Drottningholm* had already sailed from New York with Germans who had been interned in the United States, and the ship had arrived in Lisbon without incident.

Herr Doktor Bauer from the German Foreign Office was there at the station, politely wishing his Canadians a safe journey. Herr Doktor Thun from the Swiss embassy had also come to see them off – a guardian angel to the last – and had arranged for the best possible accommodation for his Canadian wards. The ever-faithful Miss Wilhjelm and Fräulein Keller appeared with thermoses of tea and coffee, and Isabel's pupil and friend Lisbet arrived in style, bearing a bottle of sherry, vintage 1911. It was a grand and glorious send-off, leaving many memories in its wake.

But according to Olga, right to the last minute there had been cause for apprehension:

Even on the morning of the 13th, there was still the possibility that something might happen to prevent our leaving. One group scheduled to leave the preceding Monday had been notified at the train depot that their permits had been withheld.

We appeared at the station at eight in the evening and found that three first-class compartments had been booked for our group of nine. Our departure from Germany was to be attended with more ceremony than our arrival. Hundreds of internees were scheduled to leave Berlin that day. Many families – separated for months – were being united. Husbands and wives who had been interned in separate camps; small children who looked in bewilderment at fathers who had become strangers; civilian prisoners caught unaware in Germany – all were now going home.

Three German escorts, assigned to accompany the train as far as the Spanish border, mingled with the crowd. Friends watched from the platform as the released internees crowded into their small compartments. Joy and sorrow mingled on the faces in the crowd.[1]

In the drama of these parting moments, the nine Canadians slated for exchange could scarcely believe that their hopeful dreams for release were on the verge of becoming a reality. Yet it was also a time of mixed feelings, particularly for Clara Guilding, the eldest of their number, who was, by then, well over sixty and had been bearing up bravely under the additional strain of separation from her missionary husband, who remained a prisoner in a German internment camp. As she climbed on board the train with her companions, she must surely have wondered whether the day would ever come when they would be reunited?

Finally, on the dot of eleven, the train moved slowly out of the Anhalter Station. They were off! Their route would take them through Paris to Bordeaux, then to Hendaye in the south of Nazi-occupied France, and from there to neutral Spain, Portugal and freedom at long last. As they retraced parts of the prison-train journey they had made in the late spring of 1941, it seemed almost a lifetime ago. Olga – ever observant – noticed that the people in France looked hungrier, and at the few wayside stations where the train stopped briefly, instead of offering gifts of food, people had asked for bread. The crops were poor and the houses dilapidated, but each hour brought the train closer to the Spanish border and the passengers' first taste of real freedom.

> The morning of June 15th our train passed through Bordeaux and at 12.20 in the afternoon pulled in to the small French border town of Hendaye. In the neighbouring Spanish village of Irun, another train pulled to the border and stopped. The German citizens who had returned on the *Drottningholm* walked across onto German-occupied soil. They were safely home. A German band struck up the national anthem. The swastika was raised. Hearty cheers greeted them, but as one of our fellow passengers remarked, 'It's all very nice, but it won't help fill their stomachs.'[2]

At the Spanish border the America-bound travellers waited a day and a half to change trains. The station at Hendaye flaunted huge banners welcoming home the Germans returning from America to the Fatherland. The Canadians hung out of their windows and watched them arrive – smartly dressed in American clothes, American shoes of real leather, and carrying American luggage. Nothing *ersatz* in sight, but for how long?

Isabel's recorded observations expand on her reaction to their journey into freedom:

> The moment we left Reich territory our train seemed to hurtle along, as if stumbling over itself to get away fast enough. Our spirits soared – until we saw the many thin little Spanish children. We had little need of the food we had been told to bring with us, so some of these poor waifs through northern Spain profited by it.
>
> Portugal looked more prosperous and at almost every station by-standers held up two fingers to us in the Victory sign. Lisbon – the one free port in Western Europe (although it had its first trial black-out while we were there) – was seething with a mixed population and was rife, we were warned, with agents and spies of

every description. We had little time to absorb its excitement and beauty before boarding the *Drottningholm* and sailing for home.

But it was not until we were truly on board that I could properly visualise the word HOME. For the fear factor dogged us to the very end of our Odyssey. When we left Berlin, the German women being exchanged for us from Canada had not yet arrived in port. I was in the British Repatriation offices in Lisbon when the final word came through from Berne that we were to sail on the *Drottningholm* the following day.[3]

According to the records of Canada's Department of External affairs, the transportation arrangements for the ten German women and one child who were to be part of this exchange involved a complicated procedure, since they would have to cross the US border in order to board the Portuguese vessel the *Nyassa* in New York. This ship, which sailed at regular intervals between New York and Portugal, would then carry them to Lisbon, and subsequently they could return to their homes in Germany. Six of these women (Mrs Elisabeth Bronny, her daughter Ruth, Miss Elsie Rieder, Miss Maria Klaasen, Mrs Lydia Anwander and Mrs Centra Haertle) had, in fact, been detained in an Ontario provincial penitentiary as political prisoners due to their rabidly pro-Nazi sentiments. The remaining women and one child (Mrs Elise Sassmannhausen, Miss Johanna Kirchoff, Mrs Elise Lange, Mrs Helena Schirra and her five-year-old son Dietrich) had been housed in various locations in Montreal awaiting their repatriation. An eleventh woman – unidentified – had evidently turned down the offer of a return to Germany, stating that she was perfectly happy to remain in Canada for the duration of the war. Her compatriots, by comparison, most probably lived to question the wisdom of their choice, but their ultimate fate remains unknown.[4]

A Royal Canadian Mounted Police (RCMP) memo dated 15 June 1942 states that room and board had been secured in a Montreal hotel for the six detainees from the Kingston

Penitentiary. They were accompanied by two Province of Quebec policewomen, and on Monday 8 June were joined by the four additional German citizens and one child currently living in Montreal. After a thorough search of all luggage, they boarded a train under police escort, and the Swiss vice-consul, a Mr Seminelli, also travelled with the party to New York as a representative of the protecting power. The *Nyassa* sailed from New York for Lisbon the morning of 13 June on precisely the date that the freedom train began its journey from Berlin to Lisbon carrying their Canadian counterparts.

On 21 June, the 'liberty ship' *Drottningholm* still remained in Lisbon Harbour, and more than a few of her thousand passengers were beginning to grow uneasy. An element of secrecy had surrounded this final sailing, and on the morning of 22 June, three pro-Nazi passengers who claimed to be American citizens were removed from the ship, which then weighed anchor early that same afternoon.[5]

Although all passengers were assigned a boat number and large cork lifejackets, the lifeboat drill held the next day could only be described as a formality. It was a virtual certainty that the white and blue *Drottningholm* with the word 'DIPLOMATEN' painted in huge capital letters on her decks would be assured safe passage. As if to advertise her presence, she sailed at night with all lights ablaze, and her position was radioed every ten minutes to all submarines, planes, raiders and other shipping in the vicinity. There would be absolutely no margin of error left for a possible case of mistaken identity.

On her fourth day at sea they sailed into a heavy fog, and in her notes Olga registers mild concern:

> Several passengers became alarmed at the steady wail of the foghorns. Rumours circulated among our group that an American battleship was in the vicinity, but the fog refused to reveal her outline. The following Sunday we passed the edge of a typhoon – something usually confined to the waters of the South Atlantic. Fortunately our ship's instruments had picked up the warning

signals early enough to change course and avoid potential disaster. Several of the passengers were able to discern the rising water spout in the distance as we passed to the north of it.

Then on June 29th we saw the first heralds of land – a flock of birds had flown out to meet us and by that night at 1.00 a.m. we had dropped anchor until early the following morning when we began moving into port. We passed the Statue of Liberty at 9.00 am.

We had come back! From a journey that took us to the South Atlantic, northward to Bordeaux, across France into northern Germany, then south to Liebenau, north again to Berlin. Then on the return journey we had come back across France, into Spain and Portugal, past the Azores and into the North Atlantic again – a full circle back to New York harbour.[6]

But beyond her joyful homecoming, Olga knew her true destiny lay not in Canada but across the broad Atlantic in the South African mission fields of Natal. She would find another ship and sail again – past minefields and submarines and raiders – to her African home of the heart. It was not long before Olga Guttormson had sought out and booked a passage on another ship for her return to Natal, where, for many more years she provided dedicated service to her mission. During these years, she adopted twin daughters whose mother had died when they were only a month old. Olga raised them lovingly as if they were her own, and lived to see them both follow in her footsteps in the nursing profession. What better testimonial to a woman of exceptional courage and conviction.[7]

Isabel records her own delight at the sight of New York and the Statue of Liberty:

On the eighth night, the lights of New York! It had been two weeks and two days from the heart of Germany to the Statue of Liberty. I strained my eyes for a first glimpse of her. My eyes and spirit relaxed after the strain of fifteen months when they found her as they had left her – straight, proud, and free.[8]

Welcome home

And so the Canadians had come full circle, and landed once again in the harbour from which seven of them had sailed 15 long months before. Unlike their fellow passengers, however, they were all refused permission to disembark until each one had been interviewed by a special debriefing team.[9] The ensuing interrogation, which had originally been set up by Lester B. Pearson in Washington, was conducted by two high-ranking Canadian diplomats, a Canadian army officer and a British naval attaché, who later noted their findings in a 15-page report. The questions directed at the newly repatriated women were designed to discover whatever useful first-hand information they could elicit concerning such matters as the morale of the German people, the effect of the bombing raids and general observations on food, clothing, transportation and, of course, their treatment as internees.

One of the observers noted in the report that all members of the team were 'favourably impressed by the lenient treatment shown these women by the German authorities and the Gestapo' – most particularly during their long sojourn in Berlin 'from September 1941 to June 1942, while awaiting repatriation', further noting that 'During this period they lived freely and under no apparent restrictions, except that they could not leave the city.' To the ears of the select interrogation team, it all sounded almost unbelievable, especially in the light of the pervasively patriotic mood within Canada, the United States and Britain and the propaganda necessarily associated with it.

In the report, Isabel Guernsey is quoted at length, and concludes her observations with a declaration of her firm and prophetic conviction that in spite of the devastating effects of Allied bombing, the Germans would hang on until 'the bitter end'. This opinion was shared by her companions, with the exception of Olga, who chose to remain resolutely silent, offering only frustratingly monosyllabic responses to most of the teams' inquiries, to the point where a notation was made that she was either inarticulate or perhaps even dim-witted. Olga had obviously decided that the questions she was being asked had already been more than adequately answered, and her inquisitors would simply have to wait and read the book which she fully intended to publish in all possible haste.

Perhaps the most perplexing question put to each of them in turn concerned their close association with a German woman in Berlin – a certain Caroline Kraus. It had somehow been brought to the attention of the upper echelons of Canada's Department of Foreign Affairs in Washington that this individual's activities were closely associated with the lives of several if not all of the Canadians while they were residing in Berlin. The description they were given of the woman in question indisputably matched that of their devoted old friend Fräulein Keller – ex-missionary in India, privately outspoken critic of Hitler, and a tenant in the house of an ardent supporter of the Nazi Party. Certainly the source of this 'intelligence' could only be someone of improbable reliability if he or she had not even managed to identify the suspect by her correct name.

Without exception, all nine women, including Olga, responded emphatically and indignantly to the intimation that Fräulein Keller had been deliberately placed in their company – a cat among the pigeons – to report on their activities. In their view, this suspicion was totally unfounded, and the proof of this lay in the fact that none of them had ever been under surveillance or had to report regularly to the police or Gestapo. Nor had their belongings ever been searched or their movements within the city been restricted to any further degree than those of the average Berliner.

The entire Keller/Krause story was patently the product of someone's ludicrously over-active imagination, yet the official report went on to discount the testimony the debriefing team had been given in Keller's defence and declared, 'It is felt that K's name should be placed on record and an attempt made to ascertain the nature of her activities.' Was it not possible that she had been deliberately placed in their midst to give the impression that the Germans were fine people, in the hope that these women would return to Canada with a favourable impression?

Fortunately, access to the report was restricted to the ministry – with copies sent to army and naval intelligence and also the RCMP – so Fräulein Keller's former sewing-circle companions would never know that their protestations in her defence had been written off as female naïveté on the part of a group of women 'with nothing useful to report'.

So much for Intelligence, but the main objective was to get ashore, and on the way to their respective hearths and homes and into the arms of their loved ones…Isabel to her parents in Vancouver, Vida to Three Hills, Alberta and into the welcoming embrace of her beloved son and daughter, Olga to her home on the Canadian prairies, Jamie to her family in Winnipeg, Kitsi and Doreen to their parents in Toronto, and Catherine Sherfe and Gwendolyne Foreshaw to Montreal. Only Clara Guilding chose to remain in the United States to live with her son and await her husband's safe return.

The weeks and months they had shared together were now a thing of the past – a common bond that would gradually be relegated to that quiet place of bygone memories. A few – such as Kitsi and Isabel – would remain life-long friends; and most probably, in her mind's eye, each of the *Zamzam* Seven would occasionally catch a fleeting glimpse of a particular incident or place, perhaps even a voice or a face and then it would be gone again – lost in the ebb and flow of everyday existence. They had lived through a unique chapter in a time out of time and emerged forever changed; yet, at heart, they were the same intrepid women who had dared to cross an ocean and survive.

Notes

Full details of all works cited here are in the Bibliography.

Chapter 1

1   David Miller, *Mercy Ships*. In 1909, the Bibby liner *Leicestershire* was launched in Belfast. The ship's most distinctive feature was her four masts, along with a single funnel. With the exception of service as a troop-transport ship during World War I, she plied the UK–Egypt–India–Burma route for close to twenty years as a passenger liner. After her sale to the Alexandria Steam Navigation Company in 1933, her Egyptian owners renamed her the *Zamzam* and she became a Muslim pilgrim ship sailing between Suez and the Saudi Arabian port of Jedda. A mosque was built in one of her cargo holds which could accommodate up to six hundred worshippers travelling on the traditional *Hajj* to Mecca. With the outbreak of World War II she was refitted for service as a passenger liner.

2   Logbook of the *Atlantis*, 20 April 1941. Report of the Captain of the *Zamzam*, William Gray Smith, to Kapitän zur See Bernhard Rogge, Bundesarchiv-Militärarchiv Freiburg, RM 100, Nr 46, S. 116.

3   See the passenger list at the end of this book.

4   Charles J.V. Murphy, '*Life* and *Fortune* men among 202 passengers rescued as Germans sink *Zamzam*'.

5   Peter Levitt, 'Family Saga 1940–44'.

6   Isabel Guernsey, *Free Trip to Berlin*, p. 3.

7   Letters of Violet Patchett Hankins to her parents and in-laws 1941–42.

8   Confiscated letter from one of the *Zamzam* passengers: Logbook of the *Atlantis*, Bundesarchiv-Militärarchiv Freiburg, RM 100, Nr 46, p. 118.

9 David E. Scherman, 'The Sinking of the *Zamzam*'.

10 Ibid.

11 Ibid.

12 Isabel Guernsey, as an aspiring journalist with a well-developed spirit of adventure, was immediately drawn to the 26-year-old Scherman, and found in him a kindred spirit during the many weeks they spent aboard the *Zamzam* and the *Dresden*. One year earlier, Scherman had been sent on assignment to London, where he shared a house with Lee Miller and Sir William Penrose. Miller's flamboyant lifestyle and her highly successful career as a photographer had earned her a worldwide reputation. Towards the end of the war, Miller and Scherman met again, when they were both assigned to cover the activities of the US forces as they occupied Munich in 1945, and Miller decided, as a lark, to be the first American woman to take a secret bath in Adolf Hitler's former villa. Scherman's lens captured her as she emerged swathed in a towel. Had Isabel known the story of this particular escapade, which she was unaware of at this point, there seems little doubt that she would have revelled in it.

13 David E. Scherman, 'The Sinking of the *Zamzam*'. After their return to the United States a few of the South Carolina tobacco-dealers demanded compensation from the government, making the case that the Egyptian liner *Zamzam* had deliberately followed a course which put her in the path of the German raider. They maintained – unsuccessfully – that this had occurred due to lack of proper precautions and with the encouragement of the anti-isolationist element on Capitol Hill. It is next to impossible to know whether their charges actually had any substance, as the matter was soon set aside.

14 David E. Scherman, 'The Sinking of the *Zamzam*'.

15 Isabel Guernsey, *Free Trip to Berlin*, p. 7.

16 Charles J.V. Murphy, '*Life* and *Fortune* men among 202 passengers rescued as Germans sink *Zamzam*'.

17 David E. Scherman, 'The Sinking of the *Zamzam*'.

18 Olga Guttormson, *Ships Will Sail Again*, p. 13.

19 Peter Levitt, 'Family Saga 1940–44'.

20 Bryan Mark Rigg, *Hitler's Jewish Soldiers*.

21 Keith W. Bird, *Erich Räder*.

22 Isabel Guernsey, *Free Trip to Berlin*, p. 8.

23 Peter Levitt, 'Family Saga 1940–44'.

24 David E. Scherman, 'The Sinking of the *Zamzam*'.

25 Peter Levitt, 'Family Saga 1940–44'.

26 Ibid.

27 David E. Scherman, 'The Sinking of the *Zamzam*'; Charles J.V. Murphy, '*Life* and *Fortune* men among 202 passengers rescued as Germans sink *Zamzam*'.

28 Peter Levitt, 'Family Saga 1940–44'.

29 Ibid.

30 Ibid.

31 Ibid.

32 This is actually an error on the writer's part, as Captain Bernhard Rogge's English was minimal at that time. Most likely it was the voice of Adjutant Ulrich Mohr that she mistook for that of the captain, since Mohr spoke fluent English and later was required to fill in as translator during discussions with various *Zamzam* survivors.

33 Olga Guttormson, *Ships Will Sail Again*, p. 16.

34 Eleanor Anderson (Danielson), *Miracle at Sea*.

35 Charles J.V. Murphy, '*Life* and *Fortune* men among 202 passengers rescued as Germans sink *Zamzam*'.

36 David E. Scherman, 'The Sinking of the *Zamzam*'.

37 Ulrich Mohr, *Atlantis*, pp. 166–68.

38 Bernhard Rogge and Wolfgang Frank, *Schiff 16*, p. 262.

39 Ulrich Mohr, *Atlantis*, p. 175.

40 David E. Scherman, 'The Sinking of the *Zamzam*'.

41 Peter Levitt, 'Family Saga 1940–44'.

42 Charles J.V. Murphy, '*Life* and *Fortune* men among 202 passengers rescued as Germans sink *Zamzam*'.

43 Wolfgang Frank and Bernhard Rogge, *Schiff 16*, p. 264.

Chapter 2

1   David E. Scherman, 'The Sinking of the *Zamzam*'.

2   Peter Levitt, 'Family Saga 1940–44'.

3   Isabel Guernsey, *Free Trip to Berlin*.

4   Katharine N. Strachan, 'I was a German Prisoner'.

5   Isabel Guernsey, *Free Trip to Berlin*.

6   David E. Scherman, 'The Sinking of the *Zamzam*'.

7   Ibid.

8   Ibid.

9   Charles J.V. Murphy, '*Life* and *Fortune* men among 202 passengers rescued as Germans sink *Zamzam*'.

10 Ulrich Mohr, *Atlantis*, p. 176.

11 Olga Guttormson, *Ships Will Sail Again*, p. 21.

12 Isabel Guernsey, *Free Trip to Berlin*, p. 1. The remarks cited almost certainly refer to the close feelings of camaraderie that had developed between Isabel Guernsey and the young *Life* magazine reporter, David Scherman, who presented her with a parting gift as a memento of their shared experiences. She describes it as 'a little curling wooden snake, carved by his own inexperienced hand from a salvaged piece of *Zamzam* oar. And on it he had inscribed, "To Mrs. G., with fond memories of the Atlantic Ocean, north & south, & Pernambuco & three boats & love."'

13 Ibid.

14 Politisches Archiv des Auswärtigen Amtes, Berlin R 41477 Bd. 1, Nr. 28.

15 David E. Scherman, 'The Sinking of the *Zamzam*'.

16 Ibid. In the 15 December 1941 edition of *Life*, a second and more extensive story by Charles Murphy about the harrowing experiences of the *Zamzam* passengers featured David Scherman's long-lost photographs held by the Nazi censors.

17 Ibid.

18 Ibid.

19 Ibid.

Chapter 3

1   In her original letter, Kathleen Levitt mentions the ship's 'bow' as part of her description, however it is most likely that this should be taken as 'the stern', from which the *Dresden*'s crew were off-loading the depth charges into the water.

2   Peter Levitt, 'Family Saga 1940–44'.

3   Isabel Guernsey, *Free Trip to Berlin*, p. 36.

4   Ibid.

5   Peter Levitt, 'Family Saga 1940–44'.

6   Ibid.

7   Isabel Guernsey, *Free Trip to Berlin*, p. 41.

8   Ibid., p. 43.

9 Ibid., p. 44.

10 David E. Scherman, 'The Sinking of the *Zamzam*'.

11 Olga Guttormson, *Ships Will Sail Again*, p. 24.

12 David E. Scherman, 'The Sinking of the *Zamzam*'.

13 Vida Steele, 'Published Recollections', Steele family archives.

14 Peter Levitt, 'Family Saga 1940–44'.

15 Ibid.

16 Isabel Guernsey, *Free Trip to Berlin*, p. 52.

17 Peter Levitt, 'Family Saga 1940–44'.

18 Ibid.

19 Isabel Guernsey, *Free Trip to Berlin*, p. 61.

20 Ibid., p. 62.

Chapter 4

1 Peter Levitt, 'Family Saga 1940–44'.

2 Isabel Guernsey, *Free Trip to Berlin*, p. 67.

3 Katharine N. Strachan, 'I was a German Prisoner'.

4 Herman Link, *Stiftung Liebenau under Director Joseph Wilhelm*, p. 44–68; *Lebenswertes Leben* (*Remembered Lives*). In the Chapel of Liebenau on 10 October 1970, a memorial plaque was installed; Joseph H. Friedel, *Gegen das Vergessen* (*Lest it be Forgotten*), p. 41.

5 Peter Levitt, 'Family Saga 1940–44'.

6 Ibid.

7 Katharine N. Strachan, 'I was a German Prisoner'.

8 Olga Guttormson, *Ships Will Sail Again*, p. 37.

9 Peter Levitt, 'A Memoir of the Sinking of the *Zamzam* and Subsequent Experiences.'

10 Katharine N. Strachan, 'I was a German Prisoner'.

11 Politisches Archiv des Auswärtigen Amtes, Berlin, R 41477, N 2345.

12 Isabel Guernsey, *Free Trip to Berlin*, p. 66.

13 Ibid., p. 64.

14 Ibid., p. 65.

15 Ibid., p. 93.

16 Politisches Archiv des Auswärtigen Amtes, Berlin, R 41477, N 2345.

17 Isabel Guernsey, *Free Trip to Berlin*, p. 95.

18 Ibid., p. 96.

Chapter 5

1 Isabel Guernsey, *Free Trip to Berlin*, p. 99.
2 Ibid., pp. 102–5.
3 Ibid., p. 105.
4 Ibid., p. 108
5 Ibid., p. 113.
6 Ibid., p. 112.
7 Wolfgang Schneider (ed.), *Alltag unter Hitler*, p. 146.
8 Olga Guttormson, *Ships Will Sail Again*, p. 42.
9 Ibid., p. 41.
10 Ibid., p. 42.
11 Isabel Guernsey, *Free Trip to Berlin*, p. 123.
12 Vida Steele, family archives.
13 Olga Guttormson, *Ships Will Sail Again*, p. 44.
14 Wolfgang Schneider (ed.), *Alltag unter Hitler*, p. 177.
15 Olga Guttormson, *Ships Will Sail Again*, pp. 44, 48.
16 Isabel Guernsey, *Free Trip to Berlin*, p. 115.
17 Ibid., p. 118.
18 Ibid., p. 131.
19 David Miller, *Mercy Ships*.
20 Katharine N. Strachan, 'I was a German Prisoner'.
21 Isabel Guernsey, *Free Trip to Berlin*, p. 135.
22 Ibid. p. 129.
23 Olga Guttormson, *Ships Will Sail Again*, p. 54.
24 Ibid., p. 56.
25 Ibid., p. 51.
26 Isabel Guernsey, *Free Trip to Berlin*, pp. 150–53.
27 Ibid., pp. 174–80.
28 Ibid., p. 179.
29 Ibid., p. 179.
30 Ibid., pp. 153–55.
31 Ibid., p. 202.
32 Sven Felix Kellerhoff, *Hitlers Berlin*, p. 157; Olga Guttormson, *Ships Will Sail Again*, p. 56.
33 Olga Guttormson, *Ships Will Sail Again*, p. 61.
34 Ibid., p. 62.
35 Ibid., p. 49.
36 Peter Levitt, 'A Memoir of the Sinking of the Zamzam and Subsequent Experiences.

37 Isabel Guernsey, *Free Trip to Berlin*, p. 162.

38 National Archives of Canada, Ottawa, RG 25, Nr 3033, B 40.

39 Isabel Guernsey, *Free Trip to Berlin*, p. 167.

40 National Archives of Canada, Ottawa, Nr 3033, B 40.

41 Isabel Guernsey, *Free Trip to Berlin*, p. 160.

42 National Archives of Canada, Ottawa, RG 25, Nr 3033, B 40.

43 Olga Guttormson, *Ships Will Sail Again*, p. 71.

44 Ibid., p. 69.

45 Isabel Guernsey, *Free Trip to Berlin*, p. 156.

46 Vida Steele, family archives; David E. Scherman, 'The Sinking of the *Zamzam*'. The health of Ellsworth Steele was much improved in the months following Vida's last visit. A few months before the Allied occupation of Germany, he withstood the rigours of a 'death march' through Czechoslovakia and Austria in the winter of 1944–45 as the Russians began their westward advance. Dr Alfred G. Henderson was removed to an internment camp in France, located just 60 km from the Swiss border. In November 1944, after a succession of adventures, he was able to escape to Switzerland.

47 Isabel Guernsey, *Free Trip to Berlin*, p. 188.

48 Ibid., p. 190.

49 Sven Felix Kellerhoff, *Hitlers Berlin*, p. 163.

50 Isabel Guernsey, *Free Trip to Berlin*, p. 192.

51 Ibid., p. 193.

52 Politisches Archiv des Auswärtigen Amtes, Berlin, R 28, Nr 25 Kanada.

53 Ibid.

54 Michael S. Cullen, 'Kriegerische Idylle'.

55 National Archives of Canada, Ottawa, RG 25, Nr 3033, B 40.

56 Isabel Guernsey, *Free Trip to Berlin*, p. 194.

57 Olga Guttormson, *Ships Will Sail Again*, p. 81.

58 Ibid., p. 82.

59 Isabel Guernsey, *Free Trip to Berlin*, p. 208.

60 Ibid., p. 211.

61 Ibid., p. 213.

62 Ibid., pp. 212–14.

63 Ibid., p. 217.

64 Ibid., pp. 218–21.

65 Ibid., p. 224.

66 Ibid., p. 225.

67 Ibid., p. 226.

Chapter 6

1   Olga Guttormson, *Ships Will Sail Again*, p. 85.
2   Ibid., p. 88.
3   Isabel Guernsey, *Free Trip to Berlin*, p. 229.
4   National Archives of Canada, Ottawa, RG 25, No 3033, B 40.
5   Olga Guttormson, *Ships Will Sail Again*, p. 93.
6   Ibid., p. 94.
7   Olga Guttormson, 'The Life and Work of Olga Guttormson'.
8   Isabel Guernsey, *Free Trip to Berlin*, p. 230.
9   National Archives of Canada, Ottawa, RG 25, No 3033, B 40.

Sources and bibliography

Archival sources

Billy Graham Center Archives, Wheaton, IL, Collection 624: Documents relating to the Sinking of the *Zamzam*

Bundesarchiv-Militärarchiv Freiburg, RM100, Nr 46: Logbook of the *Atlantis* and other documents and photos of the *Atlantis* between March and May 1941; Logbook of the *Dresden* (between April and May 1941)

National Archives of Canada, Ottawa, Department of External Affairs files relating to the prisoner-of-war exchange: RG 25, Bd. 2944, 'Exchange of Canadian Women survivors of SS *Zamzam* for German women interned in Canada – Proposals' (1941–43) and No 3033, B 40, Bd. 4190 (Parts I and II, 1941–43)

Politisches Archiv des Auswärtigen Amtes (Political Archive of the German Foreign Office, Berlin): documentation relating to the sinking of the *Zamzam* and the release of the nine Canadian women, April 1941–June 1942

Unpublished sources

Hankins, Violet Patchett, private correspondence addressed to her parents and in-laws, 1941–42, archives of Peter Levitt, Toronto

Scherman, David E., 'The Sinking of the *Zamzam*', unpublished memoir, New York, 1994, archives of John Scherman, New York

Steele, Vida, letters, photographs and memorabilia, Vida Steele family archives, San José, CA

Primary bibliographic sources

Anderson (Danielson), Eleanor, *Miracle at Sea: The sinking of the Zamzam and our family's rescue*, Springfield, Missouri: Quiet Waters Publications, 2000

Frank, Wolfgang and Bernhard Rogge, Schiff 16: *Die Kaperfahrt des Schweren Hilfskreuzer Atlantis in den sieben Weltmeeeren*, Oldenburg/ Hamburg, 1955

Frank, Wolfgang and Rogge, Bernhard, *Under Ten Flags – The German Raider Atlantis*. Translated by Lt. Cdr. R.O. B. Lang RNVR. New York: Ballentine Books, 1956

Guernsey, Isabel, *Free Trip to Berlin*, Toronto, 1943

Guttormson, Olga (as told to Jane Nelson), *Ships Will Sail Again*, Minneapolis, 1943

Guttormson, Olga, 'The life and work of Olga Guttormson', in *A History of Naicam and Surrounding Districts*, Winnipeg, 1980

Levitt, Peter, *A Memoir of the Sinking of the* Zamzam *and Subsequent Experiences: With entries from his mother's account*, Lugus, 2011

Mohr, Ulrich, *Die Kriegsfahrt des Hilfskreuzer* Atlantis, Berlin, 1944

Mohr, Ulrich (as told to A.V. Sellwood), *Atlantis: The story of a German surface raider*, London, 1955

Moore, Isabella, 'I saw Hell aboard the *Zamzam*', in *Louisville Courier* (Kentucky), 10 August 1941

Murphy, Charles J.V., '*Life* and *Fortune* men among 202 passengers rescued as Germans sink *Zamzam*', illustrated with photographs by David Scherman, *Life*, 23 June 1941

Murphy, Charles J.V., 'Prison ship: Nazi censor releases *Life*'s *Zamzam* pictures', *Life*, 15 December 1941

'Passenger list of the *Zamzam*', *New York Times*, 20 May 1941

Strachan, Katherine N., 'I was a German Prisoner', in Canadian Red Cross despatch, September 1942

Swanson, S. Hjalmar, *The Augusta Synod Passenger,* Zamzam: *The story of a strange missionary odyssey*, Rock Island, 1941

Secondary sources

Bird, Keith W., *Erich Räder: Admiral of the Third Reich*, Annapolis, 2006

Cullen, Michael S., 'Kriegerische Idylle', in *Die Zeit*, 3 July 2008

Friedel, Josef H., *Gegen das Vergessen: Die NS-Verbrechen der Euthanasie an Menschen der Stiftung Liebenau* (*Lest it be Forgotten: Nazi crimes of euthanasia against patients in residence at Stiftung Liebenau*), Meckenbeuren, 2008

Hoyt, Edwin P., 'A Second *Lusitania*: A new act of barbarism', *Sunday Express* (London), 5 July 1970

Hoyt, Edwin P., *Raider 16*, New York, 1970

Kellerhoff, Sven Felix, *Hitlers Berlin: Geschichte einer Hassliebe*, Berlin, 2005

Laprise, Andreé, 'Des civils Internés pendant la deuxième guerre mondiale: Le camp des femmes de Kingston, 1939–43', unpublished PhD thesis, Université de Montréal, 2001

Lebenswertes Leben: 'Aktion Gnadentod' in der Stiftung Liebenau (*Remembered Lives*), Stiftung Liebenau, Liebenau, 1990, published 50 years later in honour of the departed

Levitt, Peter: 'A Memoir of the Sinking of the *Zamzam* and Subsequent Experiences', Toronto, 2011, including the extensive correspondence of his mother, the late Kathleen Levitt, archives of Peter Levitt, Toronto

Link, Hermann, *Die Stiftung Liebenau unter Direktor Josef Wilhelm 1910–53*, Stiftung Liebenau, Liebenau, 1995

Miller, David, *Mercy Ships: Prisoner of war exchanges*, London, 2008

Rigg, Bryan Mark, *Lives of Hitler's Jewish Soldiers: The untold story of Nazi racial laws and men of Jewish descent in the German military*, Lawrence, 2004

Schneider, Wolfgang (ed.), *Alltag unter Hitler*, Reinbek, 2000

Slavick, Joseph. P., *German Raider* Atlantis, Annapolis, 2003

Film and internet sources

Under Ten Flags: The German raider Atlantis, film (USA/Italy), de Laurentis Paramount Pictures, 1960, director Duilio Coletti

Zamzam: *A missionary odyssey*, video (USA), Evangelical Lutheran Church in America, 1993, producer Tim Frakes

Zamzam website: http://zamzamship.home.mchsi.com

Appendix: *Zamzam* passenger list

From the archives of the Billy Graham Center, Wheaton, IL. It is incomplete, having been compiled from reports from press associations, missions throughout the United States and other sources. In some instances identification of passengers was not available.

Ambulance drivers

Butcher, George McF., 21, of Seattle, WA
Clark, Michael K., 21, of New York
Colcord, Ray, Jr, 24, of Tulsa, OK
Crudgington, James W., of Cincinnati, OH, Princeton student
Davidson, William A., 22, of Worcester, MA
Emsheimer, Henry, 36, of New York
Faversham, Philip, 33, of New York
Finneran, George C., 21, of Rye, NY
Greenough, Thomas O., 20, of Proffit, VA
Harriss, Charles L., 20, of New York
Havilland, Raymond, 20, of St Louis, MO
Hoeing, Frederick W., 33, of New York, Harvard instructor
Jeffress, Arthur T., 35, of West Hollywood, CA
King, Donald S., 25, of Chevy Chase, MD
Krida, Arthur Jr, 26, of South Kent, CT
McCarthy, Charles A., 29, of Weston, MA
Morris, John, 28, of New York
Mueller, Arthur, 32, of Butte, MT
Redgate, Robert L., 19, of Harrison, NY
Ryan, John W., 21, of Newton, MA
Stewart, James W., 36, of Oneonta, NY

Tichener, George O., 24, of Maplewood, NJ
Vicovari, Francis J., 29, of New York
Wydenbruck-Loe, William A., 50, of New York

Missionaries

Agrinson, Miss Alida, 41, of Chicago, IL, Lutheran Sudan missionary
Albaugh, Dana M., North Baptist missionary secretary
Almen, Miss Florence, of Chicago, Brethren Church missionary
Armstrong, Miss Mae P., Free Methodist missionary, Portuguese East Africa
Barnett, Dr and Mrs Arthur M., of Hackensack, NJ, Africa Inland missionaries
Barsalou, Father Robert, of Ottawa, Canada, Catholic Oblate Order missionary
Beam, Miss Mary, of Greenville, SC, Sudan Interior Mission
Belknap, the Rev. and Mrs George, of Boyne City, MI, National Holiness Society missionaries
Belknap, Miss Martha E.
Bergeron, Father Raoul, of Chicoutimi, Canada, Catholic Oblate Order missionary
Berntsen, Sister Olette, of Sudan Mission, French Cameroon
Blanchard, Miss Jessie, of Defiance, OH, Africa Inland missionary
Boulanger, Father Gerard, of St Ludger, Canada, Catholic Oblate Order missionary
Brill, Mr and Mrs Roy F., of Philadelphia, PA, Africa Inland missionaries
Brill, Roy Jr, 8, of Philadelphia, PA
Brill, Fay, 5, of Philadelphia, PA
Brill, Edith, 3, of Philadelphia, PA
Brill, David, 2, of Philadelphia, PA
Burgess, Miss Ruth C., of Hackensack, NJ, Africa Inland missionary
Buyse, the Rev. and Mrs L.J., of St Paul, MN, Africa Inland missionaries
Buyse, Robert J., 12, of St Paul, MN
Buyse, Marion, 8, of St Paul, MN
Byron, Miss Grace, of Pleasant Grove, IO, Brethren Church missionary
Charbonneau, Father Hermengilde, of Montreal, Canada, Catholic Oblate Order missionary

Cournoyer, Brother Roland, of St Bironique, Canada, Catholic Oblate Order missionary

Danielson, Mrs Elmer R., of Lindsborg, KS, en route to her missionary husband, Lutherans of the Augustana Synod

Danielson, Miss Eleanor

Danielson, Miss Evelyn

Danielson, Miss Lois

Danielson, Miss Luella

Danielson, Lawrence D.

Danielson, Miss Wilfred

Derr, the Rev. and Mrs Paul E. Derr, Assembly of God missionaries

Des Noyers, Father Bernard, of Farnham, Quebec, Catholic Oblate Order missionary

Dosumu, Miss Ayodele, of Liberia

Dosumu, the Rev. and Mrs T.O., of Liberia, missionaries

Edwards, Mr and Mrs William H., of Detroit, MI, United Christian missionaries

Elam, Miss Elma, of Madison, MO, Southern Baptist Church missionary

Engel, Mary A., 32, of Baltimore, missionary nurse

Fix, the Rev. and Mrs W. Ted, of Blountville, TN, Africa Inland missionaries

Fix, Mary L., 1, of Blountville, TN

Fredette, Brother André, of Central Falls, RI, Sacred Heart Order missionary

Gondreau, Father Phillippe, of St Pierre Batiste de Mégantic, Quebec, Catholic Oblate Order missionary

Guilding, the Rev. and Mrs W.J., of Detroit, MI, Africa Inland missionaries

Guttormsen, Miss Olga, Norwegian Lutheran missionary

Hall, Miss Barbara

Hall, the Rev. and Mrs David B., missionaries

Hall, John

Halsey, Miss Harriett, of Syracuse, NY, Africa Inland missionary

Henderson, Dr and Mrs A.G., of Winnipeg, Canada, United Christian missionaries

Hult, the Rev. R.D., of Springfield, MO, missionary

Hunter, Dr and Mrs De Graff, missionaries

Hyatt, Miss Helen, of Cape Town, South Africa, Seventh Day Adventist missionary

Jenkins, Mr and Mrs Thomas J., of Scotts Bluff, NB, Seventh Day Adventist missionaries

Johnson, the Rev. and Mrs Stanley, of Walla Walla, WA, Seventh Day Adventist missionaries

Johnson, the Rev. and Mrs Eugene, and two children, of Minneapolis, MN, Lutheran missionaries

Juneau, Father Paul, of Maskinonge, Canada, Catholic Oblate Order missionary

Keck, Mr and Mrs Claude, of Springfield, MO, Central Bible Institute missionaries

Kinnan, Miss Vemura, of Crookston, MI, Lutheran missionary

La Flamme, Brother Henri, of Manchester NH, Sacred Heart Order missionary

Landis, Miss Alice, of Elisabethtown, PA, Africa Inland missionary

La Rivière, Father Louis, of Saints Zacharie, Quebec, Catholic Oblate Order missionary

LaValle, Brother Mathias, of Montreal, Canada, Sacred Heart Order missionary

LaVallee, Brother Aime, of Central Falls, RI, Sacred Heart Order missionary

MacKnight, James P., of Allentown, PA, United Presbyterian Church missionary

McCallister, the Rev. Theodore and Mrs Florence, of Wheaton, IL, Scandinavian Alliance missionaries

Moore, Miss Isabella, of Bethlehem, KY, Southern Baptist Church missionary

Morrill, the Rev. and Mrs Curtis, of Ashland, OH, Brethren Church missionaries

Morrill, Elaine, 4, of Ashland, Ohio

Morrill, Stephen, 14 months, of Ashland, Ohio

Morrison, the Rev. and Mrs Thomas K., and two children, of Lexington, VA, Presbyterian missionaries

Muir, the Rev. and Mrs R. Nelson, of Poughkeepsie, NY, Faith missionaries

Mundy, the Rev. and Mrs W.A., of Irvington, NJ, Africa Inland missionaries

Nadeau, Brother Herman, of Providence, RI, Sacred Heart Order missionary

Norberg, Dr and Mrs C. Einar, of Minneapolis, MN, Lutheran missionaries

Norberg, Carl, of Minneapolis, MN

Norberg, Miss Marie, of Minneapolis, MN

Norberg, Miss Ruth, of Minneapolis, MN

Ohman, the Rev. and Mrs Walter A., of Cleveland, OH, Gospel Church missionaries

Oiness, Miss Sylvia, 29, of Baltimore, missionary nurse

Olson, Miss Esther, of Eau Claire, WI, Lutheran missionary

Olson, Miss Rhodie, 26, of Pittsburgh, PA, Worldwide Evangelisation Crusade missionary

O'Neal, Dr and Mrs Paul, of River Falls, AL, Southern Baptist Church missionaries

O'Neal, Miss Annette, of River Falls, AL

Paquette, Father, of Amqqui, Quebec, Catholic Oblate Order missionary

Parent, Brother Leo, of Neuville, Canada, Catholic Oblate Order missionary

Pellerin, Father Pierre, of Montreal, Canada, Catholic Oblate Order missionary

Powell, Mrs J.C., of Burgaw, NC, Southern Baptist Church missionary

Reynolds, Miss Dora, of Franklin, TN, Presbyterian missionary

Rogalsky, Miss Lydia, of McPherson, KS, Scandinavian Alliance missionary

Russell, Mr and Mrs C.A., and child, of Union Springs, NY, Seventh Day Adventist missionaries

Russell, Mr and Mrs James S., and child, of Toronto, Canada, Seventh Day Adventist missionaries

Russell, Mr and Mrs Thomas S., and child, of Hartford, CT, Seventh Day Adventist missionaries

Schwartz, Dr and Mrs Merle H., Disciplines of Christ missionaries, Belgian Congo

Smith, Dr and Mrs Paul J., of Pittsburgh, United Presbyterian missionaries

Smith, Dr and Mrs Tinsley, of Denver, CO, Southern Presbyterian Church missionary

Snyder, Miss Ruth, of Conemaugh, PA, Brethren Church missionary

Steele, Mr and Mrs Ellsworth, of Alberta, Canada, Worldwide Evangelisation Crusade missionaries

Thompson, Miss Margaret, of Monroe, OH, National Holiness Society missionary

Turner, Miss Carol O., of Hartford, CT, Africa Inland missionary
Utz, Miss Ruth, 30, of Baltimore, MD, missionary nurse
Williams, the Rev. and Mrs Robert, of Harrah, WA, Brethren Church
    missionaries
Young, Mr and Mrs Fred J., of Gestonia, NC, Africa Inland missionaries

Others

Burton, Paul A., of Wilson, NC, tobacco merchant
Cawthorne, Harry, of Wilson, NC, tobacco merchant
Conboy, Frank E.
De Liguori, Prince Alfons, Italian prince
Dreyer, Dr. N.B., Canadian
Guernsey, Mrs T.D., of Vancouver, Canada
Hankins, Mrs Violet, of Toronto, wife of a South African doctor
Johnson, Tinkie, of Raleigh, NC, tobacco merchant
Johnson, William A.
Lassetter, Mrs Elsie
Laughinghouse, Ned, of Wilson, NC, tobacco merchant
Levitt, Mrs Kathleen, of Montreal, Canada
Levitt, Peter, 6, of Montreal, Canada
Levitt, Wendy, 2, of Montreal, Canada
McWhannel, Mrs Nora O.
McWhannel, Miss Sarah
Massey, Walter E.
Miller, Thomas, of Wilson, NC, tobacco merchant
Murphy, Charles J.V., member of board of editors of *Fortune* magazine
Newman, Dr L.E., of South Africa
Pouloo, Miss Parasaphino, Greek nurse
Sallari, Miss C.T., Greek nurse
Scherman, David, *Life* magazine photographer
Smith, James, of Wilson, NC, tobacco merchant
Solnick, Paul E.
Starling, Mr and Mrs Robert A.
Strachan, Mrs K.N., of Toronto, Canada
Thompson, Miss Audrey, 14, of St Johns, New Brunswick, Canada
Thompson, Mrs. W.E., of St Johns, New Brunswick, Canada

APPENDIX

Turner, Miss Doreen, of Toronto, Canada
Uytendale, Mr and Mrs Arthur, of Belgium
Uytendale, Miss Jodelieve, of Belgium
Uytendale, Ivo, of Belgium
Wright, Mr and Mrs Dudley

Index

A   —·

B   —···

C   —·—·

D   —··

E   ·

F

G

H   ····

I   ··

J

K

L

M   — —

N   —

O   — — —

P

Q   — — ·—

R   —

S   ···

T   —

U

V   ···—

W

X

Y

Z

SOS   ··· — — — ··

CQ —·—·/ —·—
Amateur call for/request
to contact/communicate

MORSE CODE

QQQ - presence of a
suspicious vessel

R-R-R-R-
Break in & add message
then ship identity &
position